CO

Susan found herself at the threshold of true spiritual transformation. The signs? A longing that nothing external—not romance, success, money, adventure, parenting, or creating—had ever fully satisfied. This book takes us through a remarkably powerful, helpful forgiveness process that will stir your desire to awaken to who you truly are. Her well documented life experiences demonstrate love in practice. If you want a real-life account of how to undo the 'one' block to love, then this is your book.

Nouk Sanchez & **Tomas Vieira**, *Take Me to Truth; Undoing the Ego*

... Susan Dugan gives us a superb explanation of forgiveness, what it is, and exactly how to do it. I highly recommend this book to anyone who's interested in the fastest way to peace and enlightenment.

Gary Renard, best-selling author of *The Disappearance of the Universe*

This series of engaging and often humorous essays allows a peek into one woman's process as she practices true forgiveness throughout her overly-scheduled days. Her inspired determination to keep peace of mind as her primary goal provides hope and motivation for the rest of us.

Carol Howe, author of *Never Forget To Laugh, Personal Recollections of Bill Thetford*, Co-Scribe of *A Course In Miracles*.

For Kevin and Kara, with deep love and gratitude

Message from the Author

About eight years before I started studying *A Course in Miracles* and truly recognized it as my path home, a close friend and fellow spiritual seeker gave me the big blue book. Someone had passed it on to her and although she recognized on some level that it held great wisdom, she just couldn't wrap her head around it. "Read this," she said. "Maybe *you'll* get it."

Skipping the introduction and preface in my typical rush to ascend, I opened it to the first page of the text and read:

> There is no order of difficulty in miracles. One is not 'harder' or 'bigger' than another. They are all the same. All expressions of love are maximal.

My heart raced. This gigantic tome was talking about *miracles*, defined by Webster's as *"an extraordinary event manifesting divine intervention in human affairs."* As someone actively striving for years to seduce the divine into intervening in human affairs, I was thrilled. How many times had I sensed a benign presence guiding my steps? Just as I had always suspected, experiencing miracles (regardless of size) was a piece of cake once you got the hang of it. This book would teach me how to cultivate that boundless power; enable me to summon it on command. My fingers itched as if clutching a magic wand.

I continued to read the Principles of Miracles in Chapter 1 but my mind soon glazed over. Undeterred (after all, that first paragraph appeared to say it all), I decided to come back to it later and skipped ahead to the workbook. It offered 365 lessons, one for each day of the year. I could do this, I told myself, already crafting a "To Do" list of manifestations and transformations I planned to accomplish on a micro and macro level; harnessing the power of the universe to intercede on my behalf and on behalf of loved ones; creating a kind of heaven on earth right here and now on the streets of Denver, Colorado.

Oh, the folly of youth. About a third of the way through Part I of the workbook, my enthusiasm waned. Try as I might, I couldn't seem to discern the instructions for miracle making. Instead, the lessons focused on enticing me to question all I believed about the external world and my relationships. Although they contained many promising statements such as *"God goes with me wherever I go," "My mind is a part of God's. I am very holy"* and *"I am the light of the world"*, they also seemed preoccupied with the meaninglessness of my experience and overlooking the bad behavior of others; advice that smacked of denial, a habit I was trying to break. Then again, the constant use of the "G" word rankled. I preferred names unlike the unstable divinity that had so terrified me in the Catholic Church: monikers such as "universe," or even, in a pinch, "love."

Ultimately, the first time around, I just couldn't seem to connect questioning the nature of my relationships and external experience as the workbook recommended with the happiness that had seemed so elusive in my daily life. With the deep sigh I had become famous for among those who knew me best, I placed the book back on the shelf in my office beside other metaphysical publications also destined to fail me: my burgeoning library of spiritual disillusionment.

Years of seeking passed. I mastered the principle of the law of attraction enough to manifest moments of happiness and success but always the long awaited arrival of what I thought I wanted delivered only the most fleeing pleasure. Literally, within minutes of receiving a desired external result, I found myself craving the next accomplishment or resolution. Like everyone else on the planet, I also experienced profound disappointment in my relationships and career, but continued to believe that if I just pushed myself a little harder, just honed my interpersonal and professional skills a little more, just managed to manipulate some other person or situation into meeting my needs, I would achieve the result I'd been seeking. It never worked.

And so manifesting lost its luster. I couldn't seem to stay focused. I longed for something else I couldn't name: a longing I began to admit I had always carried and seemed to have come in with; a longing that nothing external—not romance, success, money, adventure, parenting or creating—had ever fully satisfied. The well of deep loneliness at my core I had buried for so long suddenly revealed itself. A person could drown there. Terrified, I called out again for help from the universe, love, whatever: that mysterious presence I had been missing so deeply and feared I had squandered as long as I could remember.

Through a series of coincidences, the answer came this time in the form of that same big blue book collecting dust on my shelf. Now I was ready to really listen, to admit I did not know; that nothing I had tried had ever worked. I found a Course study group. I started reading the text and doing the workbook again. I still craved miracles in form but eventually, admitting again and again that I did not know and asking for help from the part of my mind that did, I became aware of the critical ego in my head raging 24/7 against everyone and thing seemingly responsible for disrupting my peace. I immersed myself in the teachings of premier Course scholar, teacher, and original editor, Dr. Kenneth Wapnick. I began to understand the ego's dynamics of separation from love and apply the transformative tool of forgiveness *A Course in Miracles* offers to heal and unify our seemingly split mind in my relationships.

I eventually began to behold my addiction to uniqueness, and accept the one problem the Course identifies as the cause of all human suffering: the *belief* that we have separated from God/the one eternal love and wholeness we remain in truth. I began to gradually accept the one solution, turning our mistaken perception over to our whole mind: the part of our one mind that followed us into the dream of uniqueness and competing interests but knows the separation never happened and simply smiles at our mistaken perception. The Course calls this process of withdrawing our belief in the mistaken idea that anyone or thing outside our mind can disturb or enhance our peace forgiveness. Over time, tempted again and again to perceive myself unfairly treated, I continually asked for help from the part of our one mind that remembers our wholeness; this time to truly understand forgiveness; to learn to apply it in all my relationships; to harness its extraordinary power in an ordinary life.

Today, six years later in a class I am teaching about forgiveness, I find myself considering workbook lesson 89 in the review sections I also used to skip in my race toward divinity. "*I am entitled to miracles,*" I read, grateful for the understanding that I am entitled (with help from our inner teacher) to *change my mind* about all I believe is happening to me. Forgiving has given me a better grasp on the Course's definition of a miracle, which has nothing to do with milking gifts from the universe or coercing a dualistic God or his emissaries to intervene on our behalf.

Why did that symbol of the awakened mind, represented in Jesus, choose to call this A Course in *Miracles*? Maybe because no one would read it if he called it *A Course in undoing the ego thought system by changing your mind*. Or maybe because he knew the word "miracle" is like catnip to those of us who seek; a way to coax us in the door that we might stay long enough to let him teach us what we really want.

Defined in Dr. Wapnick's glossary-index as "*the change of mind that shifts our perception from the ego's world of sin, guilt, and fear, to the Holy Spirit's world of forgiveness;*" the miracle occurs when I catch myself following the ego's plan for salvation; holding someone or thing seemingly "out there" responsible for disrupting or enhancing my peace of mind to keep me from returning to our one mind and choosing again for truth.

The one problem and the one solution lie side by side. When I remember I am entitled to change my mind, and with our right mind's help, actually do it, I receive a glimpse of the real world beyond the clouds of guilt and judgment obscuring true vision. In that moment of perfect clarity and completeness, all longing ceases; ancient hatreds fall away; the heavy burden of this unique existence lifts, and a peace beyond all understanding—the peace of our one, true nature—resurfaces in my mind. And in ways I still cannot comprehend, but am beginning through daily experience to trust and welcome anyway, to all minds.

These collected essays represent my written journey to date with forgiveness, beginning two years after I recognized the Course as my real path home. I first published a couple in the *Miracle Messenger*, a newsletter I wrote and edited for the Rocky Mountain Miracle Center in Denver, Colorado for several years. I posted many of the subsequent essays on my blog, http://www.foraysinforgiveness.com, launched in February 2009. Others have never seen the light of day.

I began writing about forgiveness, *A Course in Miracles* style, for the same reason I began teaching the Course: to deepen my understanding, accelerate the ego's undoing, share and experience the benefits of forgiveness and help heal our one mind. It struck me, reading through these essays, that they conveyed the forgiveness process which, at first, can seem quite daunting.

Even though forgiveness does not require us to *do* anything except turn away from attacking and defending the ego's illusions and accept the Holy (Whole) Spirit in our mind's memory that we remain one with God, forgiveness is not easy. Our underlying fear of punishment for our *unconscious* belief that we chose individuality over perfect, eternal, wholeness, as well as our continuing attraction to illusory uniqueness, can make it very difficult. In mid-argument with a loved one, as we stand apparently unfairly accused, we would much rather (in the Course's words) "be right than happy." As practicing the Course raises our awareness of our attraction to and identification with the ego's sneaky ways, our pain often increases. Most of us slip into self-judgment, another form of enormous resistance. Some of these essays are reports from the eye of just that storm, accurate accounts of my own fear, paralysis and mistaken belief in and attraction to a false, ego-controlled self.

But in each case, I got through by continuing to ask for help from the part of our mind that sees only our one true self and can never fail us. And in that instant, outside time and the confines of illusory bodies competing for survival in a hallucinated world, that moment in which I no longer held another responsible for my suffering, I experienced extraordinary release from the heavy weight of this false self I drag around to defend against the truth. That deep comfort beyond all understanding really does return when we "loose" the world and ourselves from all we thought they were (to borrow another Course expression).

It struck me as I re-read these essays, chronicling several years in my journey home, that I am spending far less time in the eye of the storm and far more embracing the holy instant of release that reflects the real world, available when we have forgiven all our misperceptions. I am still at the very beginning of this excursion; but at least I am learning that blaming others for my pain hurts like hell, while releasing them allows me to smile. I hope my stories of practicing forgiveness will help shed light on the viciousness of the unreal ego thought system we have mistaken for reality as well as the deep comfort of our true, one, eternally loving nature, regardless of the path you have chosen to find your way home.

Susan Dugan
Denver, Colorado, March 2010

Introduction

What is *A Course in Miracles?*

The content of *A Course in Miracles* came to two renowned psychology professors at Columbia University in the 1960s and 1970s in answer to the painful recognition that their "must be another way" of relating in this troubled world. Today recognized worldwide as one of the most profound spiritual teachings of all time, the spiritual psychology offers a beacon of light in our contemporary darkness. It maintains that we all harbor unconscious guilt as a result of a repressed belief that we chose and succeeded to separate from the one, whole, eternal, indivisible love we share. Fearful of punishment while attracted to the idea of individuality, we attempt to project our guilt onto others to preserve our relative innocence and separate identity. This results in a futile game that condemns us to perpetual conflict.

The Course teaches us to undo guilt at its source by practicing a unique form of forgiveness in our relationships. As we learn to hold others harmless for our distress and forgive the impossible dream of uniqueness, we begin to remember the unified innocence of our true nature. Peace returns to our minds and we begin to remember God's love, the one, true love we never really left.

What is Forgiveness?

What could you want forgiveness cannot give? Do you want peace? Forgiveness offers it. Do you want happiness, a quiet mind, a certainty of purpose, and a sense of worth and beauty that transcends the world? Do you want care and safety, and the warmth of sure protection always? Do you want a quietness that cannot be disturbed, a gentleness that never can be hurt, a deep, abiding comfort, and a rest so perfect it can never be upset? All this forgiveness offers you, and more.

A Course in Miracles, *Lesson 122, Forgiveness offers everything I want.*

A Course in Miracles offers us a practical, radical process for undoing our belief in a world of attack and defense that seems to prevent us from finding permanent peace of mind. Its **forgiveness** practice has nothing to do with the world's definition of **forgiveness**: "to excuse for a fault or offense." The world's definition of **forgiveness** requires us to take the high road, forgiving the horrible thing you did to cause my suffering. *A Course in Miracles*, on the other hand, leads us to an understanding that although others may cause our physical or psychological bodies to suffer, no one can jeopardize our peace of mind because, in truth, there is only one mind that has never left its eternal, unified, loving source.

All this sounds very elevated and confusing unless you understand, allow and continually review the myth at the foundation of the Course explaining the repressed guilt that drives our every move. In the beginning there was only one. We existed eternally within the peace and wholeness of our creator. There was no division between creator and created, only infinite love. At some point, the idea of separation arose in the mind of the created, what the Course calls "the tiny mad idea," which the created took seriously. When we *believed* we had actually severed our connection with wholeness (thereby destroying our source) the one mind appeared to split. We now had a wrong mind (ego thought system) that believed we were guilty of celestial homicide and must flee from imminent punishment, and a right mind (Holy, "Whole," Spirit's thought system) that retained the memory of our true nature.

Reveling in the idea of experimenting with individuality while simultaneously terrified of punishment, the ego then pitched its plan. It would create a world into which we could flee and retain our seemingly separate identities while hiding from our source and denying our guilt by casting it outward. At this point, the one mind seemingly followed the ego into an entire projected universe of guilt and fell asleep, no longer able to

8

remember it even had a mind that could choose again for the voice of reason/wholeness.

The Course calls the process by which we learn to choose again for the wholeness we never left, **forgiveness**. It teaches us that everything we think we are experiencing outside ourselves in this dream of self-imposed exile, everything that seems to happen *to* us, is a projection of the denied guilt in our one mind. Our experience is but an external, illusory picture of continually resurfacing internal guilt that we project ("thrust outward") to prove our innocence at another's expense, momentarily relieving our torment. Once we have retaliated, however, the guilt returns, leaving us pedaling an endless, exhausting cycle of attack and defense.

Any time we feel less than peaceful we are (largely unconsciously) blaming someone or thing for jeopardizing our happiness. Everything (our ego-fueled emotions and sensations to the contrary) we seem to experience here in bodies is actually playing out in our one mind, a reflection of our denied guilt over mistakenly believing we ran away from home and destroyed it on the way out. **Forgiveness** allows us to step out of the attack/defense cycle by catching ourselves in the act of judging, attacking, or defending, recognizing that the problem is not "out there" but in our one mind, and choosing again to see things with the Holy (Whole) Spirit's gentle vision.

Our negative feelings are the red flags *A Course in Miracles* teaches us to use to recognize that we have chosen the ego as our teacher rather than our right mind. Through its unique **forgiveness**, we learn to withdraw our belief in the ego's impossible dream of competing interests, opposites and opposition. By applying this practice in our daily lives, we begin to observe how much time we spend and waste blaming others, defending our uniqueness and pushing love away. The more we recognize the pain our mistaken beliefs have cost us, the more motivated we become to admit our errors without self-judgment, and we can enjoy the gentle correction and deep comfort of choosing the wholeness that we never truly left.

As we begin to spend more and more time watching the ego's antics with the observer/decision maker in our mind and choosing wholeness again, the ego thought system gradually weakens. Our life takes on new meaning (in truth, the only meaning it can possibly have). We experience longer periods of peace and shorter periods of distress. Eventually, our belief in guilt healed, we joyfully reunite with the one love we never left.

When our minds are healed through **forgiveness**, moment by moment, the external world we perceive may or may not change; but it will no longer have any power to jeopardize our peace of mind. In this way, as workbook lesson 121 assures us: *"Forgiveness is the key to happiness."*

And now: to the eye of that illusory storm.

In the Doghouse with the Ego

We had just come home from my daughter's first high school basketball game. Her nagging cold had not responded to the vitamin and herbal remedies I kept cajoling her to take. As captain of the team she had a lot invested and felt elated by the victory, despite feeling under the weather. We drove home to the music of her picking every player's performance apart, harmony provided by my husband who could rarely resist a good post-game critique.

The low-level annoyance simmering at the edge of my conscious mind began to bubble. It had been an especially trying day with Christmas chores added to the usual burgeoning weekend "To Do" list. I had already talked with my husband who tended to over-identify with our daughter's athletic performance about advising her from the sidelines. The coach had cautioned parents against doing so at the first parents' meeting of the season, an event my husband failed to attend. What I considered his disregard for rules had been a long-standing source of conflict between us, aggravated, I felt, by our daughter's adolescence. It seemed even more important to me now that we provide solid role models for our teenager, even though, in truth, I so often fell short.

By the time I dribbled a path through the landfill of tangled lights and boxes of outdoor Christmas decorations my husband and daughter had strewn about the house that morning and settled into my spot on our sectional sofa with a bowl of stew, I felt shaky. I usually avoid caffeine but had indulged in a cup of coffee with breakfast to rev up for the many tasks at hand. My blood sugar had been zigging and zagging all day along with my mood. When my daughter popped a CD of *Christmas Vacation*—the 1981 Chevy Chase movie we use to launch the holiday, hoping the slapstick, dysfunctional family disasters will throw our more subtle variety into relief—I already had one foot in the door of my personal house of misery.

When I was three, my mother went back to work as a teacher leaving my younger brother and me in the care of a neighbor with two young boys. I used my role as only girl to ratchet my perceived abandonment up a notch—hiding for hours in a ramshackle doghouse in the neighbor's backyard. For days I sulked in self-imposed exile after our mother dropped us off, lavishing my Tiny Tears doll with all the tender care my mother seemed to have withdrawn from me. I am sorry to say that all these decades later I still now and then banish myself to the proverbial doghouse whenever those feelings of rejection rear up.

Although this movie generally brings out my inner Tina Fey, on this particular evening not even the cat taking out the Christmas tree like a feline suicide bomber could make me laugh. My husband and daughter's mirth shook my doghouse walls. Every scene seemed to mock my isolation. I didn't even remember at first to ask for help from my right mind as the practice of forgiveness has taught me to do; although a part of me did stand detached, watching like a witness at an accident scene. Now and then my daughter would sneak peeks at me, no doubt confused by my reaction to a movie she knew I had always enjoyed. To me, though, it seemed increasingly shrill as it rattled my prison walls.

After the film, I decided to go to bed, hoping to circumvent a showdown, but their voices in the kitchen trailed up the stairs to me.

"Everything Mom makes me take for this cold does nothing," my daughter complained. "Only the Nyquil you gave me works, Daddy."

"I know," he said. "None of that stuff works for me, either. You're just like me."

Their conspiratorial banter continued in this vein as I visualized all the vitamins my daughter had stuffed between cushions or dropped down heating grates over the years; the expensive Chinese herbal concoctions I'd stirred up for her only to find them congealing on a windowsill several days later. They went on to articulate other traits they shared apart from me. The door to my doghouse slammed shut behind me. I stood engulfed by my story of exclusion at the hands of my ungrateful family.

After my daughter went to bed, I attempted to let my husband have it, but—muzzled by a fury I did not understand—I ended up stomping upstairs and slipping into bed instead. Eventually I dozed off to the soundtrack of their transgressions playing in my head.

The next morning a kind of paralysis had replaced my anger. The walls of my belief in separation closed in on me; my doghouse door remained locked. I spent the next twenty-four hours running mindless errands and replaying the story I had chosen to reenact, while begging for help from my seemingly unavailable right mind. Despite having made *A Course in Miracles* my spiritual path, I found myself alone, excluded, banished, and yes, cheated by the Course. I didn't believe I could love or be loved again. I didn't even know how to make it through the day. Still, I pleaded with the Holy Spirit to help me *want* to release this sob story of unfair exclusion that had cost me everything I thought I wanted.

I have suffered from fleeting bouts of depression all my life but I don't think I had ever experienced loneliness this deep, maybe because I had never been willing to truly face it. But now something in me recognized that my doghouse was burning and I could only escape by walking straight through those flames, feeling the heat on my skin and taking responsibility for both building the structure and setting the fire. I realized I would rather die forsaken and alone than give up my story of suffering and, more importantly, my leading role in it. Still, a part of me knew there had to be a better way, and continued to cry out for help.

The following morning the fire had burned itself out. I no longer saw myself abused by my family in any way. Without further, futile analysis, I accepted how often I had acted based on this unconscious story, and thanked my right mind for coaxing me through the flames of illusion to see it as the same old problem: the belief in separation from God. And the same new solution: remembering through the Holy Spirit that it never happened.

I believed I had excluded God and tried to pin that crime on my loved ones. In years past, I might have wallowed for weeks on end without any shift in perception. But now I saw that despite the enormous pain of the last twenty-four hours, practicing forgiveness had allowed me to reclaim my peace of mind relatively fast. Suffering can motivate. It helped me release a tale of abuse I made up in childhood by clueing into my anger and despair and asking for a better way of looking at this.

Downstairs, my husband and daughter had whipped up their signature homemade waffles, cut up fruit and poured orange juice. My daughter stood folding the paper napkins so they made a little pocket for the utensils, the way I'd taught her, the way I'd learned in Girl Scout camp.

"Want to eat breakfast with us, Mom?" she said.

She leaned toward me, her back to my husband, and lowered her voice. "What is up with him this morning? Oh, my God; he is being *such* a jerk."

Republican Dreams

Lately I've been dreaming about Republicans.

The first night, I was on vacation with my teenage daughter at a beach. We found ourselves in a house much like the home of friends we used to visit each summer in North Carolina only more idyllic, transformed by dream dust into something worthy of the cover of *Gourmet* magazine.

We sat sipping lemonade from chilled tumblers, pelican wheeling outside the banked windows. A lovely young mother sat before us, her two perfectly behaved daughters coloring away on the floor. Her husband flipped through a magazine. But it was her one-year-old baby girl that caught and held our attention. She stared at us with eyes so ancient and loving they took our breath away.

"Looking at beautiful people makes her happy," her mother said.

"I know what you mean," I said, although I had no idea. She was friendly and engaging. I liked her, and wanted her to like me.

Beside me, my daughter and the baby continued their visual love affair.

"She likes to look at me," the woman continued. "I mean; I'm an attractive face. But the face she most likes to look at is George Bush."

I felt as if I'd fallen out of a tree. My daughter pressed her knee against mine as it dawned on us that we had unwittingly stumbled into enemy territory.

"She loves to watch him on TV," the father said. "Our dream

is to take the girls to see him live."

Now I was seriously freaked out. In my peripheral vision, I watched my daughter's shoulders creeping toward her ears. I awoke before I could figure out how to flee without them discovering our true identities, the baby's gaze still sticky on my skin.

The next night I found myself dangling my arm out the window of a car passing through a tunnel of undulating Georgia O'Keefe paintings toward a weekend getaway in Taos, New Mexico. On a road trip with women friends, laughing our heads off at something someone said. I don't remember the conversation but do recall the camaraderie, the sense of spaciousness without and within good friends evoke. Most of all, I remember my shock when I turned to look at the driver and the sight of Barbara Bush catapulted me back to waking consciousness.

As a Course student, I am especially sorry to admit that I have spent most of my life disliking Republicans, condemning Republicans, and feeling morally superior to Republicans (even though right out of college I found myself in Washington, DC working for one; but that's another story). Although I am no longer engaged in actively trying to defeat them, I still shy away from people at PTO meetings and cocktail parties who do not seem to share my political views. On the few occasions where I have accidentally gotten to know and like one I have concocted elaborate rationalizations, exempting us both as the exceptions that prove the rule.

Since becoming a Course student, I've spent a lot of time telling myself I no longer judge them, I wish them well, I simply don't choose to associate with them because it doesn't bring me peace. But my dreams had another version of me to share.

The Course tells us we are afraid of love. The only thing more frightening than acknowledging how much I hate you for not upholding my worldview is acknowledging how terrified I am of your love. Why? Because in truth there's nothing out there except God's love; we think we killed it, and we think it wants us dead.

If I admit that I like a Republican another chapter in the story of Susan dissolves and I imagine myself one step closer to returning to God's punishment for the tiny mad idea that I could make it on my own.

Fortunately, we have a teacher ready, willing, and able to help us see the insanity in all this. I had been asking our inner teacher for just such clarity when these dreams came and still, it took me two of them to begin to laugh at myself and let another of my "secret" thoughts of separation go. The dreams helped me see that disguising and hiding my grievance did not eliminate it. And they helped me *feel* the cost of holding on to it, the wall against love it preserved in me.

On the level of form, I still don't agree with most of the policies advanced by the Republican Party in these "United" States and am looking forward to working to put a Democrat in the White House. But on the level of truth, I know that I cannot do so from a perspective of righteousness and spiritual arrogance and still make it home. There are no separate interests and as I go about the motions of participating in this world I will ask and ask again to remember that I am here only to fulfill my special function of forgiveness, however that plays out, however long it takes, and however many Republicans and Democrats I befriend and forgive along the way. And whether asleep or seemingly awake, I will try to remember to laugh at my dreams.

Go There!

The CT scan report had bad words in it, words my doctor had not used when she told me I should not get freaked out because, really, this was no big deal. My liver did not show damage, she said. My blood work was stellar. The spots could have been there for decades; could even be a birth defect. But the CT scan report had a different way of putting it. "Malignancy/metastatic disease cannot be excluded," it said, referring to the "indeterminate" lesions incidentally found during a test to identify the sudden onset of abdominal pain. The latter turned out to be an attack of acute diverticulitis that had me recalling an early *Saturday Night Live* routine, and feeling nursing home-bound decades before my time.

"Don't go there," I thought, that day in the doctor's office as she rattled off the name of what the almost certainly benign lesions probably were, explaining I would need another CT Scan in three to six months to "confirm stability." The phrase reverberated in my head as I took the elevator downstairs to pick up prescriptions for two powerful antibiotics that would soon rob my body of every possible bacterium, leaving it vulnerable to all sorts of viruses. How did one "confirm stability" in the body, in this world based on the unstable ego thought system of separation from reality? That was something I would truly like to see.

Before finding *A Course in Miracles* I had exhausted several other spiritual paths, including my family's Catholicism, Zen Buddhism, and a variety of energy-healing, quantum-leaping, positive-thinking and law-of-attracting programs in my quest for happiness here in this body, this world. All offered various degrees of fleeting comfort, but stability? The New Age practices urged me to concentrate on what I wanted and how good it would *feel* to have it, while avoiding negative thoughts and emotions that—like runaway cancer cells—would just attract more of the same.

"Don't go there," I chanted in my head that day, driving home from the medical center, old habits temporarily displacing all I had learned practicing forgiveness as I allowed the underlying, overwhelming fear of losing this physical body and the sin and guilt it masked to have a run at me. "Don't go there," I heard a voice advising as I compulsively searched online for symptoms, causes and treatments; largely reassured by the extremely small likelihood the lesions would turn out to pose a serious threat. I obeyed the voice. I didn't go there, just as I had not gone there twice before when I'd had nasty looking, melanoma-resembling moles removed that had turned out okay. I pushed the thoughts away, replacing them with images of Susan resting unscathed, eternally peaceful, cradled in the whole love she had never really left. I didn't go there for weeks, until, at the urging of my Chinese Medicine doctor, I requested a copy of the CT scan report for my records.

I'm not sure why I expected to feel reassured when I tore open the cardboard envelope delivered to my front door. Instead, the legalistic description worked like a sucker punch to the solar plexus. Before I could stop myself, I had gone there. Fully, madly, deeply there, staring into mortality's trick mirror and no longer seeing my reflection staring back. I'm too young to die, my ego wailed. What about my family, my friends, my work? I was just starting to get this Course. What about all the forgiving I still had to do? I watched the world turning on its beautiful axis without me, struggling to force air in and out of my lungs. Impossible! I abandoned my writing project and embarked on a frantic marathon of errands and aerobically performed chores designed to keep my mind away from going there again. But I had glimpsed the ultimate, ugly, terrifying result of the ego thought system: death. And the horrific vision did not fade.

Over the next three months I began to develop symptoms. Not pain exactly but a peculiar tenderness in the liver area, a nagging awareness of the organ I could not shake even as I turned to the Course for help. A seeming attack within the body is no different from a seeming attack from without, I kept reminding myself. This is the mind on ego; I am looking at the repressed guilt of the one mind over an impossible sin. I chose to project this "attack" on this body—my body itself—to reinforce the reality of a vulnerable, individual that in truth does not exist. But I can choose again.

I constantly asked for help, conversing daily with the Holy Spirit when the familiar twinge on my right side surfaced, while the ego's dire chatter of "what ifs?" continued.

I had grown used to putting the ego's dirge on the back burner. As a student of the School of Reason for teachers and aspiring teachers of *A Course in Miracles* I had learned to put my fear of public speaking on the back burner every time I taught, turning the class over to our only true teacher, even as my heart raced and the ego prattled on about my shortcomings. School of Reason students had been independently studying healing over the summer break, with special emphasis on *The Psychotherapy Pamphlet*, *The Song of Prayer*, Chapter Five, and The Teachers' Manual. How ironic!

A Course in Miracles is a path in *undoing* all we believe about our bodies, our identities, and this world. That means *going there*. For three months, I seemed unable to distract myself from doing so. This was a gift. If we defend against our guilt/fear/negative feelings/illusions how can we let them go? We must first look with our inner teacher without judgment at the brutality of the ego thought system our belief in separation created to be motivated to release it. Workbook lesson 163, "There is no death. The Son of God is free," offers a great explanation of why we persist in believing in death (sadness, fear, anxiety, doubt, anger, faithlessness, etc.) despite the terror it induces.

The idea of the death of God...implies that God was once alive and somehow perished; killed, apparently, by those who did not want him to survive. Their stronger will could triumph over His, and so eternal life gave way to death. And with the Father died the Son as well.

Our ego mind would rather die than face the punishment we believe we deserve for offing God, even though it never happened. We could not possibly have killed God/love, and this world of sin/guilt/fear the ego invented to hide out in does not exist. But we would rather die than relinquish our grip on the illusion of separate selves, or take our projections back to the one mind where the mistake occurred and choose again for truth. The miracle reverses projection as we *go there*, bringing our seemingly large and small hallucinations back to our one mind where healing happens. When we do this, our external life may not change but our healed minds will experience only eternal peace and happiness.

And despite the "good news" that the second CT scan "confirmed stability" and the doctors' belief that these spots were harmless birthmarks, the outcome was not as important as the opportunity to forgive my desperate investment in my independence. Of course I was enormously relieved. Jesus (the symbol of the awakened mind that speaks to us in *A Course in Miracles*) is not asking us to deny our bodies; he knows we think we're bodies or we wouldn't be here. He's simply asking us to question our belief in our experience, and to consider its purpose.

I still believe in my body but that's OK because a part of me stepped back with my inner teacher and observed my attraction to the fear that keeps the illusion in place. Every time I do that, the dream grows a little dimmer; and true stability, a little stronger. It takes courage to really look at and *feel* our sin, guilt, and fear without judgment, and to ask for a better way. But, over time, it delivers greater peace. And if I can *go there*, believe me, anyone can.

Love Until Your Heart Breaks

On the phone she still sounds like a little girl. Of course, I can't see what she is wearing, but will soon enough recall the tight jeans leaving the house this morning, deliberately shredded all over to create the impression of having been fed upon by a large, rabid dog. A gauzy, empire-waist shirt with requisite plunging neckline and Hoola-hoop earrings complete the ensemble. Oh, and I almost forgot to mention, enough black eyeliner to service the cosmetic needs of the entire cast of *America's Next Top Model*.

She would be holding her cell phone and texting friends, iPod dangling from ear, I will soon think, before the next chapter in the complex story of our relationship unfolds. But for one precious moment holding the phone I hear my little girl again in her voice. And I understand completely what Mother Teresa meant when she talked about loving until it hurts because my heart is breaking and I am grateful to have loved that hard.

I have a good friend who could not have children. Back before I was even sure I wanted my own she tried fertility treatments and In vitro to no avail. Unlike some people I knew who went on trying for years, hired surrogates, or arranged expensive international adoptions, my friend appeared admirably resigned to her fate. Her only regret? Forgoing the opportunity to experience a child's "unconditional love," she said. I never questioned that assumption. My heart went out to her and I counted my blessings. At least I still had a shot at it, I thought.

In his book, *Parents and Children: Our Most Difficult Classroom*, *A Course in Miracles* Scholar Dr. Ken Wapnick shatters the myth that children feel unconditional love for their parents and amps up the shock factor by claiming they do not really love their parents at all. Love, after all, is not the same as *need* and as long as our children depend on us for their very survival their feelings for us must, at best, come with strings. We give the little ingrates what they want and need and they perform for us like trained seals; until they reach adolescence, of course, and begin starring in their own version of *The Exorcist* in their efforts to differentiate themselves from us.

Too often in the heat of combat, we fail to remember that separating from us is their job. Coming of age as an ego requires breaking away from the dreaded bodies that brought them into this world of pain in the first place and now block their path to fortune and fame. Separating from us is their job because they must reenact the original separation from you-know-who to once again prove their identities. We have all played this game. Some call it the circle of life but it is really the circle of separation repeating itself over and over again in the split mind.

Dr. Wapnick goes on to say that the very best thing we can do when our sweet, hormonally challenged progeny's head starts spinning around is lower our expectations, refrain from taking it personally, and, you guessed it, *forgive*: forgive our need to be special; forgive our need to have our child affirm our wholeness, our happiness, our spirituality, our individual worth as a good parent and human being. The very best thing we can do is watch with our inner teacher and love them anyway as they navigate the treacherous road to adulthood we have all travelled. Certain that once they have accumulated the "treasures" of this world for themselves, zigzagged down one path and another, playing hide and "seek but do not find" as the Course puts it, they too will begin to look for a better way.

On the phone my daughter still sounds like a little girl and in that moment, before my current, conflicted concept of her reconfigures in my head, I love her truly as I have never loved before without any need for a return on my investment.

An Interview with the Ego

"You're never going to get this," it said.

"Did someone ask for your opinion?" I countered.

"You've been at this for *how many* years now?"

"It's none of your business."

"How much more rejection do you think one person needs to take?"

I stuck out my tongue.

"I'm just saying."

I found myself once again at my desk chatting with the ego, even though I knew better. I had just talked with my agent about a collection of short stories she could not seem to find a publisher for. I had been writing fiction for fifteen years and, as my ego enjoyed pointing out, with the exception of publishing short stories in largely obscure literary magazines, my literary career was in the toilet. Despite having written several novels and catching the attention of three agents, my book deals always fell through. I was the poster child for the ego's mantra: "seek but do not find." You'd think it would cut me some slack.

"Just not good enough, perhaps," it said.

"I can't hear you," I lied.

"Most people would have gotten the message by now; don't you think?"

I had recently embarked on yet another fiction project that had completely stalled: the characters mouthing clichés, their conflicts murky, color draining out of the settings, my voice eluding me. In a funk, I tried to busy myself with other tasks. Fiction writing had been both blessing and curse for me: the former when I managed to stay present and allow whatever wished to express itself to flow through me; the latter when I allowed the ego to batter me about outcomes.

"What kind of example you think you're setting for that kid of yours?" it asked, moving on from my failings as a writer to my unsuccessful roles as mother, wife, wage earner, daughter, friend, person, *A Course in Miracles* student, until I could stand it no longer. I squeezed my eyes shut and again cried out to the Holy Spirit in our one mind for help.

The advice I heard in my right mind resembled the advice my mother gave me as a child when I complained about my little brother tormenting me. *Quit fighting it. It just wants your attention.* Then I remembered Ken Wapnick's advice: *look (observe) at the ego until you can genuinely smile.* And so I decided to interview the ego in hopes that granting it the limelight it craved might get it off my case, exhaust it, and maybe even leave me smiling again. I took it out to lunch at an imaginary restaurant and turned on my make-believe recorder. Here's what it had to say.

Me: What exactly do you do for people?

Ego: I am the voice within you can count on; when you need advice; when someone's kicking you in the face. When you have that gnawing burn in your gut that somebody's taking advantage of you, I'm always there to help you see clearly.

Me: Kind of like *Ask Amy* only you don't even have to ask?

Ego: Bingo!

Me: So you help people figure out whom to blame?

Ego: That sounds a little negative. Let's say I help people keep what's rightfully theirs.

Me: Like a tax attorney?

Ego: Good one. Look, this world is all about survival. You can't afford to let down your guard. You let someone cut you off in traffic, the next thing you know your children have a meth lab in the basement, the bank's foreclosed on your house, your wife's left you, and you got a God-damn brain tumor. It's a dog-eat-dog world.

Me: Can I quote you on that?

Ego: I should hope so. And try to spell my name right this time. That's Ego with a capital "E." One word—like Bono.

Me: I understand you're something of an expert on health.

Ego: I know a lot about the human body. I'm up on all the latest medical studies and trials. You can really slow down the aging process if you pay attention to your lifestyle and take the right supplements. A little work never hurt anybody either. I'm actually a lot older than I look.

Me: And yet you're really going to town on that Fettuccine Alfredo and Crème Brule.

Ego: That's because I blew it on a jelly donut and triple latte this morning. Once you've blown your diet for the day you might as well eat anything you want. I read somewhere that the human body can only metabolize 6,000 calories a day. You got nothing to lose once you reach that number.

Me: You mean gain.

Ego: Funny.

Me: So you're an all or nothing kind of guy?

Ego: You only live once.

Me: I hear you're quite the expert on romance, too. What's the secret of a good relationship?

Ego: Find the *one* person on this earth who can make you happy. A lot of crybabies come to me complaining about bad relationships when they simply chose the wrong person. It might take a while to find the perfect match but everyone has a soul mate on this planet. You just have to keep looking. You get what you give; you know what I'm saying?

Me: Only too well. What is your political affiliation?

Ego: A lot of people think I'm a Republican but actually I'm kind of apolitical. I'm more of a man behind the scenes. I take on campaigns. Mr. Spin, they call me because I can talk out of both sides of my mouth. I'm really quite talented at TV ads. You might say I have a knack for exposing Achilles' heels.

Me: What about your religious affiliation?

Ego: I'm not partial to any one path as long as you find a religion that teaches you to recognize and atone for your sins. That's the only way you're going to get to heaven. And don't even think about meditating. You won't get there sitting on little pillows with your eyes closed and your fingers pinched together.

Me: I thought you said you only go around once?

Ego: Duh—on earth! You really aren't very bright are you? You get your shot here and then you go to heaven or hell, depending on the sin factor. Didn't you ever read the Bible?

Me: How about forgiveness?

Ego: I'm all about taking the high road when someone's sinned against me. Always accept an apology, that's my motto.

Me: Right. You're looking a little tired.

Ego: Too much sugar will do that to you.

Me: Just one more question then—what do you think of the Decision Maker?

Ego: Who?

Me: The Decision Maker.

Ego: Never heard of him.

Me: He says he's known you for longer than he cares to remember.

Ego: Listen, I said I never heard of him. Believe me, I never forget a name, or a face for that matter.

Me: Or a rejection letter.

Ego: You flatter me.

I turned off the tape recorder, finished my imaginary chocolate mousse, turned back to my computer, and entered my writing space again in peace.

The ego stretched out for a long afternoon nap. It's so cute when it's sleeping. ☺

Some Things Will Never End

My teenage daughter had been chosen to sing a duet in her high school's end-of-the-year POPS concert. In his fifteen years in the role, the choirmaster had only chosen freshman for solos once before. It made my daughter feel special. I am sorry to say it made me feel pretty damn special, too.

As a very young girl, I had written plays and coerced my brothers, neighborhood children, and even an aging Labrador retriever into performing for the adults in our basement and backyard. By the time I got to high school, however, stage fright prevented me from ever auditioning for a leading role again. I resigned myself to lead singer and dancer in the chorus, all the while pining away for the spotlight I once relished. Now my karma had come full circle—enabling my daughter to make the debut my descent into shyness had preempted.

Now don't get me wrong. I am not one of those neurotic stage moms consumed with winning a spot for their weary spawn on *American Idol*. I had never pushed my daughter into anything — on the outside, anyway. In my parallel ego universe, however, I sat at a Singer sewing machine stitching imaginary costumes, my daughter's musical theatre career spinning bobbin-like out in my twisted little wrong mind.

She rehearsed at school over the next couple weeks while continuing to play her starting position on the JV soccer team through the trials and tribulations of what passes for spring in Colorado: a sky lobbing handfuls of slush one minute; unleashing a faucet of pollen the next. At one of her games, the wind tossed the goal into the air like a candy wrapper. Girls from both teams stormed the field to the rescue, wrestling it back into place like circus acrobats. The losing season forged on.

My daughter had inherited my severe tree allergies among other special qualities. Her eyes had taken on the haggard look of our neighbor's hound. Just days before her performance, I took her to her voice lesson. Ten minutes in, her voice failed and her teacher called it off. With all these voice metaphors floating around you'd think it might have registered on me which voice I had been listening to. But seduced by our promise of specialness, I had already sided with the voice for fear.

For the next three days, I obeyed the ego's instructions like a marionette, flailing and hovering over my daughter, pumping her with tea and honey, vitamins, Chinese herbal concoctions, and salt water gargles as she continued to rehearse, play ball, and struggle to complete final school projects. Two days before the first night of two consecutive evening performances, the choirmaster yanked her from soccer practice to attend the dress rehearsal. The soccer team had a game scheduled the next day, three hours before the performance. That night, my exhausted, nerve-wracked teenager climbed into bed with me, something she had not done in years. I tossed and turned in sympathy with her seeming plight.

That Thursday dawned with temperatures in the twenties. Schizophrenic moisture—alternating from snow to rain to sleet and back again—doused fields, lawns, and blossom-swollen trees. I fretted over my daughter as she left that morning. Even though I do not believe in interfering at school, I emailed the choirmaster and asked him to yank her again should the league go through with the game despite the weather. He politely explained that only performances trumped games and since she had time to do both his hands were tied.

The big night came. I sat in the audience agonizing through the entire first act, the program balled in my sweaty palm. I could barely breathe as she stepped on to the stage and began performing *Some Things Are Meant to Be,* from the musical *Little Women.* The song recounts the end of the relationship between Jo and her younger sister Beth, who is dying.

Some things are meant to be,
the clouds moving fast and free.
The sun on a silver sea.
A sky that's bright and blue.
And some things will never end.
The thrill of our magic ride.
The love that I feel inside for you.

Talk about special. I could see my daughter was nervous. She did not reach for the notes during crescendos as she normally would. Still, her voice did not crack once. She did not forget her lines, burst into tears, or, thankfully, scan the audience for my anxious face. She got through it. It was just a performance, after all. Nothing inside her had changed because her mouth went dry and her leg shook and her voice met her only seventy-five percent of the way. Her magnificence—the truth in her that had temporarily slipped my puny mind on ego—remained intact.

I sat humbled, watching at last with my right mind, the truth in us both. Our specialness faded along with the spotlight on my daughter and her friend as their lovely young voices grew still. The performance concluded with a song about the body's thrill ride and inevitable demise, unrelated to or fettered by the real love we are.

Some things will never end.

The next morning I congratulated her again, longing to say something to make up for the seeming error of my ways.

"I'm sorry if I've been kind of an idiot lately," I began.

She set her glass of juice down on the counter. Here comes Psycho Mom again, I could almost hear her say.

"It's just that I've never had a fifteen-year-old daughter before, you know?"

When she was little she would crawl into my lap, sandwich my face in her small hands.

"Remember when I was the mama, and you were the baby?" she would say, sending shivers down my spine. She still gave me shivers.

She smiled. "Fifteen-and-a half," she said.

Sainthood Interrupted

As a small child, I pursued goodness the way my weasel of a brother pursued evil. Intent on making it to the top of Santa's All Star List, I set about each morning and evening on my knees in prayer. "Make me good, Jesus," I entreated. By that I meant perfect, beyond reproach, saint-like, actually.

The Irish and French Catholics that raised me talked a lot about saints back then over pie and coffee and rye whisky. They lived and breathed at our dinner tables, and I felt destined to assume my position among them. If I couldn't have visions like my mother's namesake, Saint Teresa, or tolerate self-mutilation like Saint Catherine of Siena, I would claim the title of Saint Francis of Assisi reincarnated in female form, lover of animals and all things woodsy; gentle and kind to all living things.

I had, by age five, already inaugurated a clinic for ailing critters in the forest behind our development. What I lacked in medical knowledge and skill, I more than made up for in creativity and compassion. When the robins, butterflies, frogs, and chipmunks succumbed to my bungled ministrations, I buried them in cigar and shoeboxes in the well-appointed graveyard I'd built next door. I threw a good funeral, complete with handmade crosses, psalms, and dirges, and bribed the neighbor kids with cookies and Kool Aid to join in the mourning. But sooner or later the boys—reenacting their father's tales of World War II or Korea—would ransack and pillage my hospital, dig up the graves, and strew the tiny carcasses about for the dogs to make off with, shattering my halo. I would hunt them down and kill them if I could. It wasn't fair, I told Jesus, on my knees in enraged tears.

Why wouldn't anybody let me be good?

The neighborhood boys posed by no means my only challenge. My younger brother had presented a formidable, relentless trial since the day of his birth. God was testing me, I believed, when my brother knocked over the Lincoln Log castle I had spent all afternoon constructing, pulled out my Tiny Tears doll's eyelashes with my mother's tweezers, and shoved me as I strolled about the living room along with Miss Nancy on the *Romper Room* show. "See me walk so straight and tall," she would sing, and I would march and sing along. "I won't let my basket fall." I placed a book instead of a basket on my head to improve my posture. No matter, my brother would shove me and there went my halo again. I chased him around the house until one of us broke something and our mother sent us both to our room, even though it was always his fault.

Why wouldn't anybody let me be good?

I could fill volumes with tales of my sainthood interrupted by hooligan boys and little brothers, insensitive parents, aunts and uncles, teachers, lovers, bosses, husbands, and children over the decades. Several years into studying *A Course in Miracles*, I am finally able to see what my goal of goodness really masks. Why have I pursued sainthood? To provide a foil for your unworthiness, dazzling the known world with my moral superiority.

30

Fortunately—thanks to all those interfering loafs eager to expose the hatred beneath the veneer of my spirituality—it never worked. And I have come at last to see what a great favor my adversaries have done me.

I am ready to put my cross down. As workbook lesson 256 tells us, "God is the only goal I have today." Not proving my goodness at your expense, but returning to the part of the eternally whole mind I never left, the part of my mind where goodness without opposite reigns. *A Course in Miracles* does not ask us to prove how good we are, but to begin to see the viciousness of the ego thought system that actually drives us: the kill or be killed impulse that perpetuates the cycle of sin, guilt and fear activated by our belief that we could possibly have separated from our source.

I have come full circle. I still start and end my day by praying to Jesus. But I no longer pray for goodness (and no longer see Jesus as that guy on the cross that died for our sins). Instead, I ask to catch myself in the act of blaming everyone else for my lack of gentleness and kindness. I pray to remember that the only mind in need of healing is my own and that I heal not by polishing my halo but by reaching for Jesus' hand, *symbolically* extended by those I think have prevented me from waging the perfect day. God really is the only goal I have today, and I find him in you.

The Upside of Hip Fractures

There is a story; of course, in the ego's world there is always a story. Practicing *A Course in Miracles*, we begin to understand that our story that looks so uniquely tragic or hopeful nonetheless always springs from that same old story. In the original fiction, we have bought the idea that we have run away from the source of our wholeness, at large in our bodies in a world the ego mind created to both reflect and protect us from God's punishment for the crime of separation. In our effort to prove we have pulled off the impossible sin of individuality, while avoiding retribution, we project our repressed guilt on to other bodies or, sometimes, our own.

This particular version of the one story began on New Year's morning, 2009, in the idyllic Victorian town of Crested Butte, Colorado, mid-way through a ski vacation with family and friends. I had skied for four days on a pair of sweet new K-2s. Even though I had reverted to Eastern Standard Time to ring in the New Year the night before to accommodate my lark (over night owl) tendencies, I was tired. As my family and friends headed out to the mountain under a milky sky to a day that promised the kind of icy conditions and flat light I found especially trying, I begged off. I had been interacting with other people non-stop for five days. A self-declared introvert, I need chunks of time alone to replenish the energy spending long periods with others tends to deplete. That, too, is part of the story of Susan, a story I was about to illuminate in a new way with help from my inner teacher.

Here's the bottom line. I believed I could only find *my* inner teacher, *my* connection with the divine, the voice for love, Jesus, the Holy Spirit, my right mind, whatever you want to call it, alone. This is particularly amusing given the fact that I had been studying *A Course in Miracles* for five years, reading the text, doing the workbook lessons designed to help us apply its principles in our lives, attending and teaching classes and yet still somehow managed to miss the entire point! Unlike many worthy spiritual paths that also lead to awakening but had not worked for me, this path urges us to heal the belief in autonomy at the root of our suffering through our relationships. We don't do that by sitting on a mountaintop cross-legged with our eyes closed and our fingers pinched together. The silence we are asked to enter within has nothing to do with what appears without. We are asked to enter the silent part of our mind that remembers that the person sitting across the dinner table or chatting on the ski lift is actually the outlet provided to reestablish the divine connection we believe we severed. I heal my mind by seeing that the teenager glaring up at me, as I set a glass of juice before her, is not the problem; my belief in the original story of separation is the problem, but I can choose again with the help of the loving presence in my mind to remember that we are one.

But that morning I apparently needed a little review. I bid my friends and family farewell and decided to go ice-skating; one of the solitary pursuits I believed had helped me connect with the divine in the past. Walking over to the public outdoor rink through the hushed streets, I indulged a fantasy of Jesus walking beside me. But once I put on the ill-fitting rental skates, Jesus made a run for it. I had worn my lightweight ski socks and my bony ankles chafed against the cheap leather. Time and time again I came off the ice to re-lace the skates, stuffing tissues over the hot spots, then forging out once more to see if I could flag Jesus down.

Some local 'tweens playing hockey with someone's glove nearly toppled me several times. Still, I persevered for almost an hour, striving to reestablish my connection. Distracted by the throbbing in my ankles and the annoyance of dodging ill-mannered children, whose hung-over parents sat in the bleachers cheering them on, the blurry sense of Jesus in my peripheral vision never materialized. Defeated, I returned the skates and headed down the icy, still largely deserted streets to the grocery store hoping to find some over-the-counter sinus medication to ease the pressure settling in under my eyes. I would go snow shoeing maybe; that always helped me connect.

The local grocery store looked like it had been looted following a summer blackout in Manhattan, its shelves largely empty and ransacked, drifts of confetti swept into a corner of the linoleum floor. A boy with stringy hair and blood-shot eyes—a snow boarder, or "shredder" as we not so fondly called them—said he had no idea when fresh supplies might arrive over

Monarch Pass. "Hey, we're lucky I showed up," he said. "It's New Year's, man."

I hurried outside, and had gone maybe 200 yards when I wiped out, my legs thrown in one direction, the rest of me catapulted in the other. I landed hard on my hip, and bounced. I don't know if I had ever felt so alone. In that instant of a pain so excruciating that I could not pull air into my lungs, a terror gripped me, almost immediately followed by outrage. I glanced over my shoulder, half expecting to find the person who had surely pushed me, the shredder, maybe, or one of his kind. I didn't see anyone, of course. But I did feel the presence I had been seeking all morning, the presence of my inner teacher, the clear-eyed gentleness of Jesus. In that moment of complete surrender, I could almost see him holding up his hands as if to say; it wasn't me. As if to remind me who had chosen this; and to promise me he would help me see why if I would allow him.

A stricken looking woman in an SUV stopped and rolled down her window. "Don't move," she said. "I'll be right there." Several good Samaritans stood fretting over me. Did I need the EMTs? No. If I could just get up, walk on it; I would be all right, I insisted. They helped me up, and offered me a ride I refused. I sat for a while on a metal chair beside an old yellow dog that rested his muzzle on my knee. After a while, I dragged myself several blocks back to Elk Avenue, taking baby steps on the slick sidewalks, through tunnels of plowed and shoveled snow, my mittened hands pressed against the glass of store fronts selling books and high-end pottery, jewelry, and kitchenware for balance, my favorite little prayer playing in my head: *help me, help me, help me.*

Eight blocks later back at the rental, I peeled off my ski pants, filled a plastic bag with ice, popped some ibuprofen, and grabbed the Course, asking my inner teacher to show me what I needed to know. I opened the book to Chapter 21, The Responsibility for Sight:

This is the only thing you need do for vision, happiness, release from pain and complete escape from sin, all to be given you. Say only this, but mean it with no reservations, for here the power of salvation lies:

> I am responsible for what I see.
> I choose the feelings I experience, and I decide upon the
>   goal I would achieve.
> And everything that seems to happen to me
> I ask for, and receive as I have asked.

Deceive yourself no longer that you are helpless in the face of what is done to you. Acknowledge but that you have been mistaken, and all effects of your mistakes will disappear.

As in the instant when my body hit the ground I saw that I had created this, that I had already been feeling unfairly treated, my peace somehow jeopardized by these others. The fall merely reflected a belief in my victimization. Although my ego mind raced forward wondering what would happen if I had really damaged this body, how I would make it to scheduled client meetings, get my daughter to all her activities, rewrite my novel, launch this blog; the presence of my inner teacher helped me accept responsibility for my mistaken projection. As I did, I understood that this was all in my best interest. However it played out, I would be okay. The truth in me had nothing to do with another installment in the adventures of Susan's body. The truth in me could not be threatened, broken, or destroyed. As I picked up the phone to call my husband, a part of me had to smile because I had finally gotten the quality time with Jesus I craved.

That connection with the awakened mind we all share has not gone away. In the weeks that followed, confined to crutches or a walker, my husband and daughter and friends stepped up to care for me in ways I never would have otherwise allowed and a funny thing happened. As my relationship with them became less identified with the rigid roles I had scripted for us and I allowed myself to receive their love in whatever ways they offered it, my connection with my inner teacher continued to strengthen. It did not go away when my husband entered my office and began talking to me while I was writing or on the phone. It did not go away when my daughter lay on the couch watching a reality TV program involving wealthy, potty-mouthed teenagers I sometimes longed to kidnap and reform. It did not go away when clients changed their mind about what they wanted from me several times an hour. It did not go away when I studied the crumbs and dust accumulating on the hardwood floors I could not manage to sweep one-handed.

It did not go away because it can't go away. It can't go away because it never left me. It never left me because I never left it. I learned from my hip fracture that I really don't want to be alone ever again, even though I might sometimes need to close my office door to finish a project, or take a yoga class or meditate to clear my busy mind. I want to be in constant relationship with my inner teacher, the only real relationship available. When I forget it is there, I find it again by listening to the terrible loneliness of my belief in separation, the loneliness I begin to recognize and heal when I truly and with complete attention begin to listen to you.

8 reasons to make merry

I can only look back in gratitude at a few of the unexpected perks of the last few weeks:

I got to be right. I just *knew* something was broken despite the ER doc in Crested Butte's X-ray, the X-rays at Kaiser (medical center), and the orthopedist and physician assistant's advice to resume my regular activities, pain permitting; which caused me to work out on the Nordic track and take a few excruciating spins on stationery bicycles on a broken hip for crying out loud. But at least I got to be right. Better right than happy, my ego always says.

Crutches with crampons. I am not making this up. I got these crutches in Crested Butte. At the scene of the crime, dude, so to speak; just in case I decided to climb a fourteener or something. Or feel like slipping off the Course wagon for the duration of my recovery and whacking somebody who has just taken the last close-in parking space at the grocery store upside the head. (Of course, my doctor has given me a form to apply for handicapped parking but you have to show up in person at Motor Vehicles on crutches to get it which must be listed somewhere in the *Divine Comedy* as a separate circle of hell.)

Husbands and children remember how to cook. When the doctors at Kaiser finally discovered I had a fracture, three weeks into this little journey in forgiving my belief in the body and told me I had to stay completely off my leg or risk emergency surgery, my husband and daughter threw a little impromptu fondue party. They trashed the kitchen and used every dish in the house, but managed to clean up. Mostly. Except for the counters and floor. But I'm not seeing that well these days either, so what the heck. As long as I keep my socks on I'm chill. (My daughter hates it when I say that.)

Racing around on hardwood floors in your walker. This is actually a lot more fun than you might think. I go from my office to the kitchen to the foyer and back again hundreds of times a day. I call the hall between my office and the kitchen the Panama Canal because of the tight fit. The walker has a little drawer in case you want to pack a lunch or something, and a seat in case you're felled by the sudden onset of depression. It has brakes too, should you get going too fast or decide to take it down a big hill. I took it outside once but the wheels are puny. (I wonder if you can get mountain bike tires.) So I just keep racing around inside. I dream of one day making it to the living room and the television set but that big step down continues to thwart me. Anyway, that's why God made crutches. Okay, maybe not God. Who did invent crutches anyway? Couldn't they come up with something better after all these years?

The bozo horn on my cane. I'm not sure you call it a cane. I'm not sure what to call it. My husband came home with this device that has a four-pronged base and a curved handle. His employees gave it to him for his fiftieth birthday. It has a little Bozo the Clown horn to cheer you up or frighten small children. It reminds me of something the dirty old man in the old *Laugh-In* show might carry. I am dating myself. Really, I was just a little kid when that show came out. I am not even close to being ready for something like this. Not even in private. OK, maybe the horn. Just forget about it.

Someone else gets to take out the garbage and recycling. My family members look at me the way I used to look at the Holy Spirit when I first started the Course, as if at some kind of stinking Fairy Godmother, in this case a trash fairy who visits in the middle of the night to rid the house of unsightly debris. *Fairy's on vacation people—your turn!*

People carrying things for you. When I am with my friends and family, they carry things for me—my purse, my books, my shopping bags. They dote on me and even appear to agree with me more, interrupt less, etc. This may be the closest I will ever come to testing the life of the royals. I could get used to it, really.

Small children think you're a robot. I was in Starbucks on my macho crutches the other day and these two little kids were absolutely taken with my hardware. I made robot faces at them and they hid behind their mother's legs.

You Can Wake Up!

In the dream within a dream I am paralyzed by an overwhelming, unidentified fear, moaning and writhing in my bed. A part of me must be watching because I can see and hear my prone body, even as I fully inhabit its horror. The room I am in transforms. Even as I remain trembling in my own bed, the part of me that watches now sees three beds configured like a cross. I am lying perpendicular to the bed at the head of the cross. Another bed, my mirror opposite, lies directly perpendicular to mine. As I continue to writhe and call out, the part of me that watches becomes vaguely aware of my husband asleep in the opposite bed, my teenage daughter awakening in the bed at the head of the cross between us. She begins calling out to me.

"It's OK, Mom." She sits up, extends her hand. "Mom. It's OK. You can wake up."

She is a singer, my daughter, with a strong, resonant voice that finally penetrates the part of my mind enveloped in the nightmare. I begin to awaken; sit up. She continues calling, extending her hand. I lean forward and reach out to grasp it.

"You can wake up," she repeats.

Her fingers close around mine with the complete trust of a newborn's. And I become aware that the hand extended no longer belongs to her, but to Jesus—the manifestation of the awakened mind—or rather, that their hand is one. The realization catapults me awake in my own room in my real bed, heart racing.

"You can wake up," comes the voice in my head. And I realize that my daughter's *voice* and the *voice* of the awakened mind are also one.

This dream is a gift from the memory of truth and wholeness

in our one mind: the sure, still voice always calling to me from outside the nightmare of this world. It reminds me that extending my hand to those I am most apt to believe I love—and hate when they fail to meet my needs and expectations—is the means for my awakening.

"You can wake up," calls the voice from beyond the dream of this existence. And I am blown away; although I have been trying to do what this Course asks, I have never seriously entertained the possibility that I could actually wake up, become more peaceful; possibly, but actually wake up? Not in this lifetime. And yet.

"You can wake up."

The voice is my daughter's, my parents', my husband's, your voice, and mine. The voice is our one inner teacher's, the one voice that always knows what it's talking about and never, ever lies. It speaks to us 24/7, whether we're paying attention or not, and its message is *always* the same.

"You can wake up," (because you never really went to sleep). Yikes!

He Dropped Dead

"He dropped dead," said the stranger beside me at the local Japanese diner. He sat as if in prayer, leaning forward over the counter toward a woman who appeared to be the owner and clearly recognized him.

In my peripheral vision, I took in the blur of his physical attributes: African American with gray-flocked hair, probably in his late sixties, a little overweight, eyes saucer-like at the tale of his friend's sudden demise.

He clung to the Japanese woman's fingers as she listened. His friend, another regular customer who had often sat right here beside him at this very counter, had dropped dead of a heart attack a couple months earlier.

"You remember him?" the man asked.

"Of course."

The friend never took care of himself. He wouldn't take his blood pressure or cholesterol medication. He ate cheeseburgers. He would never walk anywhere.

In contrast, the man sitting beside me had lived a clean, healthful life since undergoing bypass surgery twenty-five years earlier. He stopped smoking and drinking, gave up meat. Although he went on at some length to share the steps he had taken to protect himself from dropping dead, too, he did not sound convinced.

"He dropped dead," he repeated, speaking into the church of his steepled fingers.

The Japanese woman nodded.

"You remember him?"

"Of course."

I had come here to work on a writing project that had suddenly stalled, mysteriously deprived of the nectar of inspiration that had kept it humming along for a while, once more deluded by the ego's crafty ways into thinking that venue had anything at all to do with my internal state of mind. As is often the case, I realized I had gone seeking my forgiveness curriculum in the blank page only to find it sitting right beside me.

Another, younger waitress set a bowl of rice and vegetable tempura before her regular customer; refilled his green tea.

"He dropped dead," he told her.

The friend's daughter had found her father lying in his apartment on the floor. He had been there for days—dead alone on the floor right where he had dropped for days. His daughter had called to see if the man beside me wanted her father's car, an old BMW purchased during a mid-life crisis many years earlier. His friend had wanted him to have his car. He still couldn't bring himself to drive it.

"You remember him?"

"Of course."

I sipped my tea. It was hard to swallow. I had been studying the section of the Course in Chapter 19 called The Obstacles to Peace that explores our devotion to our physical and psychological bodies, the bodies we hallucinated when we accepted the ego's lie that we had separated from our oneness and deserved punishment for our "sin." According to this underlying myth at the foundation of *A Course in Miracles*, the repressed guilt we feel over our alleged crime, combined with the continued appeal of our bogus individuality, keeps us perpetuating a story arc of birth, physical and psychological pleasure and, ultimately, suffering and death that both horrifies and enthralls us. For months I had been watching the ego thought system, threatened by the Course's truth, attack my body, hell-bent on proving its fearful reality. Even as I asked for help from my inner teacher, the part of my mind also currently activated in the stranger beside me sat in absolute shock that a person it loved could die. And, most importantly, that its own body that appeared to house its spirit might at any moment meet the same fate despite its best efforts to do the right thing.

I recalled an interview with a locally famous dance instructor I had conducted for a newspaper article I'd written. The dancer had grown up in Mongolia and escaped massacre by a warring tribe with his family only to end up in Europe imprisoned in a Nazi camp before American liberation and immigration to New York and eventually Denver. Despite the horrific trials of his early life, in our interview he kept returning to the death of his brother, followed by his own recent brush with mortality.

"He dropped dead," he said, again and again. I had given him my fingers to cling to. "I almost died," he said, over and over, speaking of his heart attack. His eyes looked like I imagined the man's sitting beside me in the diner would look if I dared to catch them head on: pupils like black holes; confidence in anything and everything shattered.

How can a world exist without you? How can a world exist

without me? The Course's answer is always the same. What world? The dualistic world we projected when the mind split is no more real than the bodies we projected and continue to project to populate it. And yet, we so covet the idea of our unique identities, and so fear the fantasized retribution of a wrathful God we invented that we continue to believe in the vulnerability of the physical shell we seem to inhabit. No matter how much we read about and try to remember our oneness, when confronted by a loved one's death or our own catastrophic illness we cower in fear, and cling to our identities as if they could offer dear life, as if they could offer any life at all.

In the final section of The Obstacles to Peace we learn that our identification with the body, our paradoxical fear of and attraction to pain, is answered in the holy instant in which we call on the memory of wholeness in our mind to help us look at the denied guilt we project on our bodies; attacking another's, as I do when guilt surfaces and I believe my daughter or husband have failed to meet my expectations, ignored my feelings, or deliberately undermined me; or attacking my own as I do through sickness, injuries, aging, and ultimately death. We can't get out of here and home to God alone. We must look at the relationships seemingly in our face. We must recognize the underlying guilt over the one true problem expressing itself again in an attack on your shell or my own, and choose again for our right mind.

By watching our negative feelings arise day in and day out, moment to moment, and returning them to the light of the right mind, our belief in what your body seems to be doing to me, or my body seems to be doing to you or to me begins to fade. Eventually, we will stand hand and hand at the threshold of the oneness we never left, ready once more to allow the magnificence of our true nature; completely certain that we give up nothing by disappearing into the one eternal love, and instead find everything that seems to have been missing for such a long time in this dream of specifics that never has a happy ending.

The man at the counter beside me asked for wasabi and finished his lunch, staring out into the space that seemed to have claimed his friend, thinking about a car parked in his driveway he may never be able to bring himself to start. I wanted to ask about his friend, let him cling to my fingers if it would help. But a part of my mind still believes I don't know him. I gathered up my pad and pen, paid my bill, plunged out into the cold, slipped into my car, and drove home.

There Is Nothing To Fear.

> You gain strength, courage, and confidence by every experience in which you stop to look fear in the face...The danger lies in refusing to face the fear, in not daring to come to grips with it...You must do the thing you think you cannot do.
> Eleanor Roosevelt, *You Learn By Living (1960)*

In sixth grade, my math teacher summoned me to the board from the back of the classroom to solve an algebra equation, unwittingly triggering a lifetime of self-doubt. I walked the plank between my fellow adolescents' desks, dodging spitballs and catcalls. I had grown eight inches over the summer and could barely place one enormous foot in front of the other without falling down. The miniskirts then popular would not sit straight on my narrow hips, puckered seams and zippers routinely slipping 60 to 90 degrees from their intended locations. My tights would not stay up; my Twiggy haircut would not lay flat; the chalk numbers and letters swimming in front of my eyes refused to synchronize. My mind went blank. Sweat pooled between the place I still prayed breasts might one day debut; the rhythm of my heart aligned with forbidden hard rock cadences.

For years, my prepubescent disgrace continued to drive me. In a couple of advanced college English seminars requiring verbal presentations, I took zeroes rather than risk a similar debacle, compromising my GPA. As a young public relations professional forced to attend a variety of conferences, I endured debilitating panic attacks every time we had to go around the room and introduce ourselves. Required to undergo media training and serve as an administrative spokesperson during a massive, statewide hospital strike, I nearly expired. When an opportunity to teach children creative writing years later presented itself— something I longed to do despite my disability—I relied on a video camera to prepare and rehearse, along with relaxation and self-hypnosis techniques to keep a lid on my anxiety.

Two years ago, when I enrolled in the School of Reason (SOR), a newly established school for teachers and aspiring teachers of *A Course in Miracles*, the ego felt obliged to raise a few salient points about my qualifications. Teaching children was one thing, it said, but teaching adults? And not only teaching adults but teaching them *A Course in Miracles*? Are you serious? Real teachers had been studying this Course for decades. Real teachers had a talent and passion for the spotlight. Real teachers knew what they were talking about. I stuffed the ego's assertions back in the trapdoor in my mind where they belonged. We were still in our first semester. No one had mentioned teaching yet. Maybe they would forget about that part. *Not.*

The school decided to offer its first student-taught class. Teachers-in-training would alternate presenting over the next year. The Jack-in-the-Box ego sprang into action. My nervous system performed its little meltdown. I could not go through with this.

Help me, help me, help me, I pleaded.

I attended counseling sessions with the ego in Holy Spirit's clothing. The stand-in for my right mind had plenty of ideas. Hypnosis or EFT (emotional freedom techniques) could help. Meditation, relaxation, essential oils, beta-blockers… My anxiety only increased.

At loose ends, I decided to actually try doing what the Course suggests. I stopped conversing and started watching. I reminded myself that nothing outside my mind was the problem; my *belief* in the ego's story of separation was the problem. I asked for help from my right mind to see things differently. After a while I opened the Course to the Introduction to Part II of the workbook, and received this promise from our one, right-minded inner teacher:

I am so close to you we cannot fail.

In that moment of awakening to truth, my terror vanished. I understood that my fear arose from believing this identity, this personality, could bring the Course's message to others. When in fact, only vacating this identity, this personality, could allow the Course's message to reach other minds, just as only vacating this identity, this personality, had allowed the Course's teaching to now and again reach my mind. In this dream of separation there are two teachers—the ego and the Holy (whole) Spirit—and one student: the mind that believes it separated, but can nonetheless learn to choose between them. If I am allowing my inner teacher to use this body for its only rightful purpose—communication—then I am not being my usual, ego-driven, terrified self, but rather expressing what the Course calls true humility.

Workbook lesson 48 reminds us that we have nothing to fear:

The presence of fear is a sure sign that you are trusting in your own strength. The awareness that there is nothing to fear shows that somewhere in your mind, though not necessarily in a place you recognize as yet, you have remembered God...

Fear of teaching this Course (or writing about my experience practicing this Course, for that matter) is really only the fear of learning there is nothing to fear. This seeming individual self I so valiantly defend actually prevents me from remembering and experiencing the one love I am. It's OK to rehearse, meditate, or sip an herbal concoction to calm the body down. But when I allow the part of my mind that knows what it is to express itself my fear of the possibility of failure vanishes.

I have only been practicing this Course for five years, not nearly the decades of some great teachers I have had the privilege of learning from. But I come to the teaching with a deep longing to know, and a deepening understanding that I don't.

Fear and Forgiveness in Las Vegas

The woman sitting at the nickel slot trailing a rubber oxygen tube from her nostrils stabbed at the air with a cigarette as the results of her last wager failed to line up. Her other liver-spotted hand patted her Barbie doll bubble cut before once again lifting a plastic cup of a fluorescent liquid to her matching lips.

She might be pushing eighty but was more likely too close to my age for comfort. I first spied her yesterday morning carrying my Starbuck's back to our room following my walk. I spotted her again as I criss-crossed through the casino to make a dinner reservation at one of the celebrity chef palaces set in a fake European city, following lunch with my husband and daughter overlooking our hotel's faux river, lagoon, and wave pool. I saw her again at 10:30 p.m. on our way home from a show, still tethered to life support, still sipping her red dye #2, bubble cut askew, still stabbing at the air with her cigarette over her latest wager's failure to line up. Sunrise, sunset; Vegas style.

What is it about this town that makes me want to pat myself on the back for my upright ways? Everywhere I look the ego is seeking but never (permanently, at least) finding, while having the tragic time of its life. And even though I know the Course says there is only one ego projecting the illusion of a story out there; here where the illusion becomes a caricature of itself I am nonetheless tempted to believe I am somehow better than my fellow seekers just because gambling doesn't happen to be one of

47

my addictions. (Not to mention tempted to believe there is more than one of us out there seeking and never finding, or anyone "out there" at all.)

Workbook lesson 71 tells us that "Only God's plan for salvation will work." We don't believe it. Vegas—like the larger dream we are all dreaming—offers the ego's alternative plan, the plan we have all bought into, a plan that revolves around judging others (after first having judged ourselves for the alleged, impossible crime of separating from God in the first place).

> It maintains that, if someone else spoke or acted differently, if some external circumstance or event were changed, you would be saved. Thus, the source of salvation is constantly perceived outside yourself. Each grievance you hold is a declaration, and an assertion in which you believe, that says, 'If this were different, I would be saved.' The change of mind necessary for salvation is thus demanded of everyone and everything except yourself.

I find it easy to see the ego's plan scribbled on the faces of the people who have come to this town seeking solace in the wheels turning on the crap tables, or the patterns changing in the windows of the slots. I find it harder to see the ego's plan of "seek but do not find" in myself. We have come here for my daughter's spring break, lured by cheap airfares and hotel deals designed to help offset a recession-ravaged season. The discomfort I have felt here all week, a low level anxiety I have blamed on the energy of all that seeking and finding around me, only reflects my own investment in the ego's plan. I have once again forgotten what I am, seduced by noise, lights and seeming chaos—the undertow of my unfulfilled expectations—into believing that my peace depends on my external, rather than internal, condition.

The truth is I have come here with my own version of the ego's agenda, hoping to resurrect my illusion of the perfect family, a vision that involves my husband and daughter performing like the trained dolphins at Siegfried & Roy's Secret Gardens and Dolphin Habitat. Instead, they sleep in late as they always do on our vacations. Instead, I slip away to walk and grab breakfast on my own as always, returning to find them still in bed watching endless *Sponge Bob Square Pants* reruns or tuned Zombie-like to a channel that—talk about illusions—plays only movies set and themed in Las Vegas! I am a lark and they are night owls. I am neat and they are slobs. I am organized and... I want to connect and they... I silently recite our differences, anti-affirmations driving me deeper into the dream, alone again, the story of my life.

Forging out through the casinos, I feel once more like the only one on this earth who doesn't get this world and its idle promises. As I head out to the pools and manicured landscaping to claim a lounge chair and lick my wounds in the brilliant sunshine, a forty-mile-an-hour gust of wind, on its way to delivering a blizzard back home in Colorado, nearly knocks me down. I can't even manage to catch some rays, for God's sake. I am close to tears before I remember to choose again, calling on the Holy Spirit, the part of our one mind that holds the memory of our one truth.

Such is the ego's plan for your salvation...For what could more surely guarantee that you will not find salvation than to channelize all your efforts in searching for it where it is not?

I have to smile. I sit for a while bundled in towels listening to the music of my right mind, watching graceful palms bend to accommodate the gale, particles of white sand dancing across a fake beach, electrically generated turquoise waves curling on a cement shore. Back in the room, my family members have miraculously risen, showered, dressed themselves, and re-strewn their belongings around the room. "Want to grab some lunch, Mom?"

my daughter says.

I touch her hair; she has beautiful hair. For once, she presses back against my hand.

That night we go to see *Jersey Boys*, a rock and roll review based on the life of Frankie Valli and the Four Seasons. Toward the end of the show, the Frankie Valli character reflects on the twists and turns of his tumultuous life, comparing his present success to a sudden break in the oppressive summer heat that plagued his childhood in New Jersey. You wake up to a blue sky and clean, crisp air and you feel whole and alive again, he says. His life was like that for a while, everything flowing with the group, making money again, healing his relationship with his partners and his daughter. When he was young someone told him: "This, too, shall pass." But he was learning that all good things pass, too. In the next scene his daughter dies of a drug overdose. *"Fallen angel, I'll forgive you anything/You can't help the things you do."*

This, too, shall pass.

The show ends with the Four Seasons' induction into the Rock and Roll Hall of Fame in the 1980s, and closes with the song, *Who loves you?* They used to play that song at the pool in our town park when I was little. I hear it now in a whole new way.

> And when you think,
> The whole wide world has passed you by.
> You keep on tryin',
> But you really don't know why...
> Who loves you pretty baby,
> Who's gonna help you through the night?
> Who loves you pretty mama,
> Who's always there to make it right?

The love we are is always there to make it right if we can get over ourselves long enough to allow it. We are forever loved; always have been. Not by the romantic, unpredictable love of pop songs but by what lies beyond our illusions: the real love we are and have never left, the only love there truly is.

People stand and cheer, stamp their arthritic feet and sob. Sixty-something women claw at the stage. I cry in solidarity. Even my husband and daughter, the youngest person in the house by far, hoot and holler. We are one; always have been. Nothing outside us can change that. For a few moments in a Las Vegas theatre on the cusp of spring, I remember there is nothing to fear, nothing I need to fix or fill me up. My mind heals as I accept the love we are flowing through actors impersonating The Four Seasons, and an audience appreciating them. It is almost worth having *"My eyes adored you"* stuck in my head for the next five days. Almost. ☺

Random Ego Thoughts on Las Vegas:

Currency: You play penny, nickel, and quarter slots but you can't use pennies, nickels, or quarters anymore, although they tell me the machine simulates the sound of coins rushing into your hands when you win (I wouldn't know). Expect to pay thirty percent more than you would in Denver at the good restaurants, fifty percent more for drinks. Just pretend it's a different currency—another kind of Euro good only at imitations of Venice and Paris—and you'll get used to it.

Treasure Island: Women in underwear on one ship versus pirates with canons on the other. Entranced children watching. Don't even get me started.

When the fun stops: A brochure advertising a 12-step program for compulsive gambling available beside a bank of slots in The Mirage, conveniently located right next to the brochure: *The House Advantage: A guide to Understanding the Odds.* (I got the last one of those.)

Twenty-something men: Still drunk enough from the night before to think you are, too, scaring the hell out of you on your morning walk with attempted high fives.

A guy named Luigi: Tony Soprano's mother's long-lost love child—staking a claim with his mortified 'tween daughter in a reserved cabana at the pools.

"But Dad, we need to pay to be in here."

"Forget about it, baby."

24/7: *Serious* drunks, *serious* bling, *serious* techno, *serious* second-hand smoke, and enough blinking lights and winking chandeliers to induce your very first seizure.

Siegfried & Roy's Secret Gardens and Dolphin Habitat: A Green facility? Really? The dolphins seem cheerful enough (their trainers insist they do not perform—this is a *research* facility—we merely exercise them) and the golden lions and white tigers downright docile but, I mean, this is a zoo after all. A zoo in the middle of a Las Vegas hotel. Green? Am I missing something?

Open Season

Yesterday I was in Las Vegas, the last of a five-day vacation over my daughter's spring break. Our flight back to Denver didn't leave until 7:35 p.m. so I headed down to the pools early while my husband and daughter did their TV thing, hoping to pull my wild thoughts about the trip together into something resembling an essay.

After I staked out our territory—three lounge chairs in a semi-secluded alcove nestled beside manicured palms on a fake white sand beach—I realized I had forgotten my sunglasses. As I returned from yet another trip up and down brassy banks of elevators to collect them, the wind tossed my folder of writing ideas I had inadequately anchored with a book about screen-writing into the air releasing its contents. For a moment, I watched the last decade of my scribbled thoughts—a confetti of yellow legal pad papers, torn envelopes, youth soccer schedules and theatre programs, café and cocktail napkins—take exuberant flight. Oddly suspended, as if enchanted by Mickey Mouse to the tune of the Sorcerer's Apprentice in *Fantasia*—clearly, it was time to get out of Las Vegas.

A mother with two teenage daughters sprang to the rescue, rushing around between the narrow aisles of largely still vacant lounges to retrieve the scraps of my haphazard spiritual journey. I followed, balling the papers up against my heart, hugging them to keep the crafty wind from whisking them away, even as a part of me wondered if maybe I should just let them go.

When we had retrieved them all, I thanked my helpers and headed for the restroom. On a marble counter I ironed them flat with my palm and stacked them back into the folder. Outside again, I spent the next half hour pruning and reorganizing, plucking and rearranging to better fit the design of my current patch of growth. The following entry seemed newly relevant:

In our miniscule Denver backyard it is once more open season for starlings. Our cat's fantasies of bagging one of them have finally manifested. Daisy does her Sphinx impersonation in the grass below the pitched eaves of our 1890 Victorian where the pigeons roosting last fall managed to defy her serial killer urges. The starlings will not be so lucky.

Today she drags a young specimen through the dreaded hatch of her cat door. Carrying a laundry basket to the washing machine in our mudroom, I interrupt the slaughter, leaving her prey trembling but merely several feathers lighter for the encounter.

The thing is the bird won't fly out the mudroom door. Even though I've propped it open and left her alone, she refuses to leave her perch on the rim of a hanging spider plant that's seen better days. My attempts to herd her toward the escape hatch a few feet away only induce a hysteria I am tempted to join. The bird flaps away in the other direction toward windows long ago painted shut, circles downstairs toward the pile of rubble of a root cellar we call the "monkey hole," where Daisy is sure to return and finish the job.

I stand watching, helpless, entranced. I cannot say why my eyes fill with tears.

"You're looking right at it," I whisper. "Freedom. Just hop through the freaking door."

The bird clings to its perch, heart hammering against the wishbone of its chest; afraid to see what's staring it right in the face; afraid to risk, claws fixed in a death-grip on the rim of plastic planter.

It is possible I suppose to die of fear, possible for birds and humans, too. And I wonder what opportunity I am looking straight at and still cannot see. And whether I really have the courage to flee the safety of my roost long enough to find out.

I wager I wrote this at least several years before finding *A Course in Miracles*, five years ago. I guess the jury's still out on flying through the door, but at least I have finally managed to leave my roost. And I am learning that fear is the only thing it is possible to die of.

Where in the World Is God?

For the last few days I have been searching for God again, as if he were outside me somewhere, as if he knew anything at all about this crazy world. I thought I almost contacted him the other night before my husband and his colleagues descended to spread out, cook dinner, and watch the NCAA championships. I went looking for him on a walk around the neighborhood but a conversation I didn't know how to have with my daughter kept playing like a stuck song in my head. He was not in the lilacs opening their embryonic fists in our front yard or the Black Hole of a baby's eyes I free fell into at the specialty grocery store.

He was missing from my morning contemplation and later at a meeting with clients. I did not find him while driving on I-25 or listening to a friend who had just learned her position with a company she'd worked for eighteen years had been eliminated. He did not show up at my daughter's soccer game, where the opposing team scored two goals in the first five minutes and the world's most mellow coach took our girls to task in a booming English accent that left parents cowering in the bleachers. I could not find him in a friend's inspiring story of her recent struggle with breast cancer. I briefly forgot about his defection while enumerating my grievances on the phone with a dear friend and fellow Course student, but it boomeranged back as I argued with my husband over the cat's continued adverse relationship with our carpets.

By even mentioning the G word, I realize I am violating an unspoken taboo among many of my contemporaries who also turned their backs on the religions of their childhoods, and, in so doing, adopted their own names for the object of their spiritual longing. Spirit, Higher Self, Love, Wholeness, Oneness, Being-ness, Is-ness, I Am-ness; you've heard them all, too. But I am tired of the linguistic charade. Let's stop mincing words here; we're talking about God, for heaven's sake, whatever that may mean for you semantically.

For me, it used to mean an indescribably larger, eternally powerful version of a human being—benevolent and malevolent, humane and vengeful—just as wacky as the rest of us only indestructible, omniscient, and thereby terrifying. The Catholic God of my childhood made decisions about life and death, sickness and health, prosperity and poverty. He had allowed the Holocaust and the invention of the atomic bomb, ran Jack Kennedy for president and allowed his assassination, killed off my aunt, grandfather, neighbor's mother, and a string of pets without warning in rapid succession, and governed everything from the weather to geological, astronomical, economic, and sociological forces.

The God of my childhood punished and reprieved according to a set of rules I could never get my head around, rules that included a detailed hierarchy of where people went after death. Sometimes according to their sins and sometimes according to situations over which they had no seeming control, such as those unlucky enough to be born non-Catholics, babies who died before receiving the sacrament of Baptism, or people who croaked without a priest around to deliver the Last Rites.

When I walked out of the Catholic Church at age sixteen during a sermon on abortion that featured a slide show of unborn fetuses, I hoped to close the door on that God for good. But I could not close the door on the God I sensed beyond the Church's God, a compassionate, sane presence I longed for but could never fully embrace; a God without opposites, a wholly loving being that would never punish his children; a being that saw beyond the suffering and insanity of this world and offered lasting peace.

Studying *A Course in Miracles* has helped me remember and recognize that non-dualistic, all-knowing, all-loving God. It also has helped me understand why I have so much trouble accepting his love. According to the myth upon which the Course's thought system relies, God created his Son (and that includes all of us) as a part of him. At some point the one Son wondered what it would feel like to separate from his Father. Although an impossibility, the Son of God believed his "tiny, mad, idea," catapulting us into a state seemingly outside heaven's wholeness.

At that point, the one mind of God's Son appeared to split into the ego, the part of the mind that believed in the separation, and the Holy Spirit, the part of the mind that knew it was a bunch of hooey. Seeking to reinforce itself, the ego convinced the Son of God he had pulled off the impossible and killed his Father in the process. Frightened that God would somehow rise from the dead to punish him, and still seduced by the promise of autonomy, the Son of God's mind fused with the ego's as he followed him into a projected dualistic world of separate, finite bodies complete with sensory apparatus designed to verify the illusion of *external* reality while preventing us from ever returning to the one mind. When our repressed guilt over what we think we've done arises, we project it outside ourselves, blaming other bodies, situations, and the ego's God for our distress; reenacting that original fissure; unable to hear the Holy Spirit or Voice for God's healing message: *It never happened.*

We believe it did. We invented a God with human attributes; a deity that seeks to blame and punish his children; an unpredictable, unstable, insecure nut case made in our image to protect our bogus individual images. And although most of us don't even know we have a mind beyond the body's brain when we start the Course, the underlying guilt over our alleged crime continues to haunt and terrify us. Fortunately, so does our deep yearning to return to a dimly recalled state of perfect, eternal peace. A part of our mind knows we are a part of God, essentially and eternally loving. Trouble is we want to return to God and retain our individuality, too, no matter the cost. And so we decide again and again that God has forsaken *us*, even as we try to cajole him into the world to help us stave off our loneliness, the disease eating away at our body, the affliction gripping our child or parent, the bill collectors pecking at our door, the wars ravaging our world and mind.

Enter the Course's practice of forgiveness that reminds us that although God is never here in this dream of separation, we are never outside the wholeness of God, despite our continued hallucination. By looking honestly at our projections with the Holy Spirit—the part of our mind that remembers the truth—we undo our belief that we are victims or perpetrators, and gradually release the barriers we have erected to keep the love we are away.

"We are as God created us," the Course reassures us again and again.

We remember this not by trying to prove how spiritually evolved and loving we are, but by noticing and facing how much we want to blame the others we invented for destroying our peace in a desperate effort to coax God into smiting them instead of us. God is not here in this dream world of ours and never will be, thank God! But we remain in God's mind, and can experience the love we never left whenever we catch ourselves in the act of judging, recognize our projections merely reflect the one problem of believing we separated from God, and turn them over to our right mind (another synonym for the Holy Spirit) for healing. As the Introduction to workbook Review I tells us:

> You will yet learn that peace is part of you, and requires only that you be there to embrace any situation in which you are. And finally you will learn that there is no limit to where you are, so that your peace is everywhere, as you are.

When I remember to stop listening to the ego's 24/7 podcast and ask for help from the memory of wholeness in our one mind, I can stop looking "out there" for peace. I can give thanks that God is not here in this dream of exile, because I am always resting in God.

I Am Missing My Daughter Again.

For days she has been in one of her moods. I tiptoe around her, reminding myself this is what sixteen year-old egos are supposed to do, the adolescent version of the separation we all keep reenacting in this dream to prove our feeble, fragmented existence.

When my husband asks her what's wrong, her head snaps around toward the sound of his voice.

"I'm in *pain*," she says, before heading back to her room.

She blames the pain on a finger jammed on a soccer ball earlier in the day. But it is the pain we all share, the pain in my husband's eyes at the sound of her exasperated response, the pain of her leaving us in slow motion the way children must in the world the ego designed to prove to us that we really have run away from home.

I have been missing my daughter for a long time now. For

years after her birth I loved like I was running a marathon. She consumed my thoughts as I sat in meetings or worked on my computer, afraid I would miss the first time she rolled over or formed a word. Later, I imagined her sitting on her little mat at the Montessori school counting out beads or shuffling the diphthong cards. There were tickling marathons that resurrected moments of perfect joining I had never experienced before. Everyone says they come back to you eventually and yet...

Even though I know *A Course in Miracles* tells us we have never left the love we are, I am missing my daughter again, as if she were something outside me I could lose or lack. To be a parent means loving without limits or prior restraints. It also means allowing your heart to be broken. That is the opening we come to again and again, the holy instant in which we turn in our pain to our inner teacher and ask to see things differently. Our children are our saviors in this way. They break our closed hearts and minds open to let in the healing light.

And yet, I am missing my daughter again today, unable to do much more than watch my craving for the object of my affections to return the favor, unable to fully accept what the Course tells us we are really missing. Mute with longing. A part of me still clinging to my special story, resisting the only real love there is, the love we are still at home in, dreaming of exile. Siding for now with the ego, bereft and unwilling to choose again.

What World?

When I left the Catholic Church at sixteen, I thought I had renounced my relationship with an unstable God. I didn't understand that the mere recognition that my religion could not satisfy my spiritual longing (although it appears to have satisfied the longing of people I love) was actually the first step away from my belief in the separated mind, and toward the wholeness we never really left.

Following a period of agnosticism and ultimately disappointing political activism, I began to explore New Age possibilities. Abundance was big business in Northern California in the 1980s. I dabbled in a potpourri of vibration-raising, energy-healing, quantum-leaping, law-of-attracting techniques designed to make my life and the world in general a living paradise. They advocated engaging the Higher Self, spirit guides, and angels to solve specific problems and enhance wellbeing. I enjoyed the meditation and the sense of something "out there" willing to intervene on my behalf. But even when I got the parking space, the job, or the relationship, my elation never lasted. Lying awake at night, I still yearned for a nameless, abstract union.

Studying meditation at a Zen Buddhism center helped me transcend the constant barrage of negative thoughts that continued to plague me, and begin to redefine my perception of the external universe. During three-hour sessions seated on little, round cushions, I sometimes reached a state of temporary euphoria and clarity far greater than what I experienced in my morning runs. But I could never get the hang of the rituals; bowing the wrong way in temple; accidentally knocking things over. For several years, I foraged through a variety of liberal Protestant denominations in an effort to offer my daughter religious grounding; but despite welcoming communities, I continued to feel like an imposter, and a lonely one.

My whole body buzzed when I opened *A Course in Miracles* to the first page of the text—having skipped the Preface and Introduction in my hurry to ascend—and read:

> There is no order of difficulty in miracles. One is not 'harder' or 'bigger' than another. They are all the same. All expressions of love are maximal.

Even though I took the word miracle literally and had no idea what those words really meant, I knew I had finally found my true path. Chills ran down my spine as I continued to read the

Principles of Miracles in Chapter 1. What a deal. With the Course, it seemed, I could find God and have my transformed world, too. The Holy Spirit was at my beck and call.

The trouble was that concentrating on coercing the Holy Spirit to address my specific concerns prevented me from applying the practice of forgiveness in my relationships and allowing the undoing of the barriers we have erected to keep the love we are away. That is the Course's real gift. Had I read (and understood) the Introduction and the Preface, I might have saved myself some time. Fortunately, I had also begun the workbook designed to undo the ego thought system by applying the Course's vision to everything outside me that seems to jeopardize my fragile inner peace.

Over time, studying the text, going through the workbook, learning to forgive my projections and judgments and to ask the true Holy Spirit—my inner teacher, the part of my mind that remembers our wholeness—I am beginning to experience moments of true joining, glimpses of the joy always available to us. The ego thought system is ingenious and relentless in its defense. As the one learning to choose against the ego and for the Holy Spirit in my mind, I must remain at least equally vigilant.

Enter the question that comes up for many Course students about whether or not the Holy Spirit helps us in the world we think we inhabit: an unreal place the ego's perception made to keep us from ever getting back to the one mind and choosing instead for truth. The question surfaces for me as the ego relentlessly tries to find loopholes in the fabric of the path I have chosen to lead me home. When it does, I find it helpful to review the Course's underlying mythology.

Jesus or the Holy Spirit (the loving presence that remains in our one mind even though we believe we fragmented) does not help us in the world because the world itself—like the objects and bodies it appears to contain—does not exist, a vital fact we have forgotten in an effort to make the dream real. Our true identity, on the other hand, exists eternally within the wholeness of the one mind we never left. Our fantasized experiment in running away from home never happened. But we subconsciously believe we pulled off the impossible and—like naughty children deserving punishment—projected the dream of this world into which we seemingly fled to avoid our source's retribution.

The world we see reflects the "tiny mad idea" of separation. (It is no more real than the bodies I perceive *out there* attacking me and other bodies, or the body I think is seeing them.) When we believed the seeming error, the one mind seemed to split, and we bought the ego's case for the story of sin, guilt, and fear that supports our individuality versus the Holy Spirit's response: "It never happened."

Given that scenario, you would think the ego would deplore the idea that God knows about the world. But the ego's cunning plan involves making God the bad guy in its drama. The ego tells us the father we metaphorically killed by choosing individuality will somehow rise to punish us, proof that we have established separate identities worth destroying for our collective crime. This is the myth playing out in our split mind: the insane lie that governs our thoughts and behavior and keeps us attacking and defending.

The Holy Spirit is not the answer to healing our mind. Our dawning awareness that we have the power to remember the Holy Spirit's peace, to take responsibility for having chosen the ego in the first place and choose again, is the answer to healing our minds. If we become dependent on the Holy Spirit's favors, we just have (what the Course calls) another "special relationship" going. Relying on the Holy Spirit for worldly favor is ultimately self-defeating, and simply drives us deeper into the dream. Identifying more and more with our role as the one mind that chose the ego but can choose again, puts us back on a path headed home. That's why the ego wants us to focus on everything but the one mind where healing occurs. In the moment we choose to see that your body or my body is not the problem, our choice to accept the ego's lie is the problem, the ego vanishes. And choosing again from moment to moment undoes the separation by removing the blocks we have placed between the chooser in our mind and the one love we never left.

While the Course does say that Jesus meets us where we think we are and *The Song of Prayer* pamphlet does talk about the lowest rung of the ladder home, where we start by asking for specific help; continuing to ask the Holy Spirit or Jesus for help in this world keeps us indefinitely stuck at the bottom of the ladder. Asking for specific help becomes a crutch that merely reinforces a journey through an unreal world made to hide the guilt in our mind. It won't lead us home.

We can't let go of that hidden guilt until we are aware of it. We must recognize our hatred for others as our hatred for ourselves before we can allow the eternal love it seems to mask. When we see the Holy Spirit through the ego's lens, our vision goes all Disney and we conjure a superhero to grant our every earthly wish. Those pastel images bolster the ego's belief in the fleeting pleasures of this dream. But they will never satisfy our deep longing to awaken to joy, to answer enduring love's call, to mend our fractured mind.

We need to ask the Holy Spirit, our loving inner teacher, to help us look at the projections/illusions we have made to hide our guilt over a separation that never happened. We need to ask the Holy Spirit to help us look at the viciousness of the world the ego made. We need to offer the Holy Spirit the one real fear we all share, the fear of the one love truly practicing the Course leads us to. With the ego as our inner teacher, we would rather punish other bodies or our own than acknowledge the insanity we created. We would rather suffer, sicken, and die than give up the illusion of individuality.

The habit of listening to the ego is strong in us. Our resistance to letting go of our seemingly separate selves—despite the Course's teachings about the cost of maintaining them—is enormous. Still, as Jesus reminds us again and again, our enormous tolerance for pain does have limits. Ultimately, we reach a point where we want out of the dream more than we want in. Really. A lot of the time. More and more each day as we remember to look with our inner teacher at our choice for the ego thought system and choose again, the practice the Course calls forgiveness.

And yet, I continue to resist. There are times when I want the Holy Spirit to fix my body or someone else's, to resolve my seeming troubles with my child or spouse, to get me that new contract, to end the wars I see out there, to take away my fear. When I do, I am learning to give the Holy Spirit or Jesus my hand. And to remind myself the hand is only a metaphor I eventually won't need if I keep practicing forgiveness and am finally able to let this hallucinated self go. There is no hand, no body, just the light in my mind that has never stopped shining. I can open my eyes on it whenever I am ready: when I am finally able to stop attacking my identity and yours in a desperate effort to prove myself superior, inferior, victorious, victimized, autonomous and finite; when I am finally able to stop asking the Holy Spirit to make real a dream of expulsion from love.

When I choose to allow the healing of my mind like this from moment to moment, sometimes my experience in the world changes and sometimes it doesn't. My relationship with my spouse may or may not improve. My diseased body may or may not heal. But whatever the circumstances of my external life, they no longer disturb me or keep me from expressing and receiving the love I am.

What is the role of the Holy Spirit in this world? When we choose to truly listen, the answer is clear, and deeply comforting: What world?

It's Only a Movie

I had almost made it to the finish-line of an ostensibly conflict-free day. Having slept fitfully the night before, I had adjusted my "To Do" list downward to include a minimal itinerary: editing a writing project, working out, brief business meeting, running errands, and cooking dinner. Now I lay on the couch oddly immersed in an *E* special chronicling the hidden conflicts on the set of the 1980s sitcom *Growing Pains*. (I don't know how the remote in my hand sucks me into these wormholes, but I do know my ego loves waxing nostalgic for the seemingly idyllic domestic fictions popular in my youth, before I married and had a child, before I started practicing the Course, before I began to admit in rare moments of clarity that there are no conflict-free days in the ego-directed production in which we all star, regardless of our marital or parental status.)

Before they could get to the bottom of Kirk Cameron's "real life" born-again conversion or Tracey Gold's eating disorder, my daughter came home from another soccer team bonding event. I hit pause, and rose to go over the plans for the next night's prom one more time. Our initial negotiations had been sketchy, and I hoped to finalize things not only with my daughter but also with a couple of other parents.

The evening's schedule for the group of thirty teens sat on the kitchen counter awaiting verification. It called for parents to descend paparazzi-like on their spawn at a nearby lake to snap outdoor photographs. A hired party bus would then transport kids to a downtown restaurant for dinner, and then on to the prom at the art museum. The bus would pick them up after the prom and take them to the after-prom event. Following after-prom, the bus would take them to the home of one of my daughter's friends, where the girls would sleep. Right!

As I reviewed the plans with my daughter, I learned two disturbing facts. First, the kids would not be *locked in* during after-prom, as I had originally understood. Second: "We probably aren't going to after-prom now anyway," my daughter said, perhaps thinking to reassure me.

The anxiety percolating on the back burner of my wrong mind, ever since a junior boy I did not really know showed up on our doorstep to invite my sophomore daughter to the junior/senior prom several weeks earlier, rose to a frantic bubble. My daughter went on to explain that the bus would probably now take the kids to her friend's house directly from the prom at about 1 a.m. where they would "hang out" until dawn.

The ego mind tallied the ramifications of these new developments: thirty kids (mostly juniors and seniors), one mother, a dozen available automobiles, immeasurable opportunities for poor choices and life-shattering consequences. I told my daughter I did not feel comfortable with this turn of events. She accused me of not trusting her. I tried to explain it was the other kids I didn't know, the many nameless and faceless unknowns I didn't trust. She raised her voice. Why couldn't I ever trust her? Why did I always assume the worst? I went completely ballistic.

Roused from his office by the crescendo of our discussion, my husband attempted to mediate. I won't bore you with the details of how well that went for him. Although I had clearly lost my mind, I made several overtures at defending my position with them both before retreating to my bedroom.

A part of my mind watched as I begged for help to truly believe that my daughter and my husband were not the problem. The original decision to side with the ego's belief in separation— a decision I kept unconsciously acting out in my relationships— was the real problem; the alleged fear for my daughter masking the real fear we all share over a belief that we deserve punishment had triggered my anger. That fear had been stalking me long before the seeming external circumstances configured to justify an attack. Still, I could not let it go. But the part of my mind that watched could remind me that I had been here before. True love—the one love we truly are—had not forsaken me. It lay just on the other side of the tempest I had created to eclipse its reflection.

I lay awake a long time, agonizing over my meltdown, terrified I had widened the gap between myself and those I most loved, all the while watching with my inner teacher; still clinging to the special conflicts that seemed to make the story of Susan real; to protect the uniqueness of this identity despite the costs.

The next morning I awoke thinking about the sitcom *Growing Pains* (ha!). About the way we get sucked into our fictions. About the steps of forgiveness that invite us to take our projections back to the projector in our mind and view them with the help of the memory of truth we all carried into the dream. When we pick up the remote and rewind like this with the help of our inner teacher, we begin to see the illusory nature of what seemed so painfully real. We begin to see it is only a movie. That it makes no sense to defend or attack images projected on a screen. Or to judge ourselves harshly for believing what our bodies' eyes were made to see and thereby strengthen: the ego's at once triumphant and woeful tale of running away from home. As Chapter 30, Section VI., The Justification for Forgiveness reminds us:

> Anger is never justified. Attack has no foundation…You are not asked to offer pardon where attack is due, and would be justified. For that would mean that you forgive a sin by overlooking what is really there…

The Course is not asking us not to get angry. Jesus knows we're angry most of the time, whether we're aware of it or not. He simply urges us to look with him at our anger's real cause and allow his gentle, awakened vision to transcend the illusion of separate interests that led us to defend and attack in the first place. In the holy instant in which we admit we do not perceive our own best interests and align instead with the loving presence ever shining in our right mind; the credits role and the seeming circumstances of our illusory distress dissolve.

> Salvation does not lie in being asked to make unnatural responses which are inappropriate to what is real. Instead, it merely asks that you respond appropriately to what is not real by not perceiving what has not occurred.

I thanked my husband for trying to help. I apologized to my daughter for my misunderstanding (error in perception), and went over the plans with her again. I called her friend's mother to make sure she felt OK about having the kids over, and offered to be on call.

I had made my daughter a book for Christmas filled with "coupons" for treats we enjoyed and could do together— shopping vouchers, chick flick movie marathons, lunch at favorite restaurants, Mom's indescribably delicious chocolate chip cookie bars. She cashed in a prized Mom/daughter manicure/pedicure and lunch ticket and we spent a few hours together. We laughed over the fashion police arrest photographs in the celebrity magazines, and at each other's hyperbolic responses to the pedicurist's tools (we both have overly sensitive feet). Later, I watched her climb on to the party bus with near complete confidence. She had promised to call us from the landline when she got to her friend's house. She had a good head on her shoulders. I silently wished her an Emmy-Award winning special, an evening that lived up to her expectations.

My husband and I stopped for dinner on the way home, both unusually quiet, contemplating how on earth we had come to a point of seeing our daughter off to her first prom. At home again, I slumped back down on the couch and hit the remote on the *Growing Pains* documentary to see if I could get to the bottom of that born-again conversion and tragic eating disorder.

The Way I Fly in Gratitude

Last night I attended an orientation for the International Baccalaureate program my daughter would officially begin as a high school junior next year. The evening started with a presentation on early college planning, delivered by the director of Post-Grad Education, the part of the guidance department charged with helping students through the college selection/application process. People laughed nervously as the woman described one of the power point slides, a cartoon illustration of a helicopter hovering over a stick figure child, introduced by the caption: "Don't Be a Helicopter Parent."

I was familiar with the term. When our daughter hit middle school and my delusion of successful parenting took a nosedive, my husband and I attended a series of *Love & Logic* parenting classes encouraging people to back off from swooping down helicopter-like to manage their children's lives. Of course, I never did that, my silently smug ego pointed out. I had always given my daughter plenty of choices to encourage her to take responsibility for her own decision-making process and its consequences. But, in truth, as she matured and the stakes rose along with the consequences, I could feel the breeze of the chopper in my head revving for liftoff.

The Post-Grad director shared some specific examples of ways in which helicopter parents, however well meaning, sabotaged their children's growing independence. Some wrote or heavily edited student's application essays. Others asked all the questions of Admissions Officers during college tours and orientations. One mother actually moved into the dorm with her child for a couple of months before the college could figure out how to evict her. (I am not making this up.)

I squirmed in my seat. Although I had never and would never take such overt measures to secure my daughter's place in the world, I nonetheless had already embarked on a little fantasy of volunteering in the Post-Grad Office, sharing my wisdom with my daughter's peers while becoming an expert on the subject of university rankings and financial aid packages. Along the way, unearthing that jewel of a liberal arts campus, I envisioned nurturing my child's fine mind and all-too-rapidly approaching future.

The helicopter cartoon jolted me back to my senses. Really, what was I thinking? Anyway, I could not "rescue" my daughter if I wanted to. After all, she had been a virtual no-fly zone from the moment I gently lay her down on her quilt on the carpet at three weeks old, walked across the room to answer the phone, and turned to find her rolling across the room toward the door, already on to bigger and better things. The first day of Montessori preschool, instead of seizing my legs and bellowing in terror over our impending separation like normal children, she high-fived me and dashed toward the playroom. She was done with bottles, done with baths, done with dolls, done with Mom's French toast and packed lunches years before I was. For a long time, I secretly took her accelerated passage through human development as an affront, fortifying a sense of rejection I had carried all my life. But I am learning little by little, practicing *A Course in Miracles*, to see (experience) things differently.

My daughter's refusal to allow me to fix up her world has helped me practice the process of forgiveness at the core of this path I say I want to learn, yet so frequently resist. I am beginning to see that nothing "out there," including my special relationships, can affect my peace of mind in any way. Only I can forfeit that, and I often choose to. I choose to in order to reinforce the pitiful story of Susan as the victim of the world she experiences, even though, as my inner ego parent constantly reminds me, my troubles pale in comparison to the troubles of many.

Often, I forfeit the truth of what I am by choosing to reinforce the story of Susan as luckier than others. How many times when people have asked after my daughter have I shrugged and said that in the spectrum of teen problems my worries are few, and for that I am grateful. Grateful I have experienced less pain than others and sometimes grateful to momentarily (at least) have experienced more; grateful that whatever my experience of suffering or triumph it proves I am really here in this unique body living this unique, unpredictable set of circumstances— better than or worse off than you.

In workbook lesson 195, "Love is the way I walk in gratitude;" the Course offers us another kind of gratitude:

> You do not offer God your gratitude because your brother is more slave than you, nor could you sanely be enraged if he seems freer. Love makes no comparisons. And gratitude can only be sincere if it be joined to love. We offer thanks to God our Father that in us all things will find their freedom. It will never be that some are loosed while others still are bound. For who can bargain in the name of love?

Who can bargain in the name of love? That would be my mind on ego. I (the part of my mind that chooses between the ego and the Holy Spirit) learn how to withdraw my investment in the heart-wrenching bargains of my special relationships by shifting my perspective from blaming or congratulating you for my feelings of inferiority or superiority, to recognizing the underlying guilt over a belief in separation from love that never happened: guilt that drives me again and again to seek both solace and revenge *outside* my mind.

In the moment I turn my perceptual error over to the inner teacher in my mind for correction, I reunite with the one love we are and have never left, and rejoice in true appreciation. I am grateful when I remember from moment to moment through the process of forgiveness that the ego's dire story of offing God through our declaration of independence is just a murder mystery my right mind has already solved. Then I can smile gently at my daughter's declaration and my own, and cut the engine on my imaginary chopper.

There is no one "out there" to rescue or get into college, no one out there to vicariously live through my unfulfilled dreams or spare my numerous mistakes, only my own mind in need of joining with the one love it never left. I find my ultimate innocence when I recognize with my inner teacher my wish to change my autonomous daughter as my own impulse to protect an autonomous identity that has only brought me pain.

> We have been given everything. If we refuse to recognize it, we are not entitled therefore to our bitterness, and to a self-perception which regards us in a place of merciless pursuit, where we are badgered ceaselessly, and pushed about without a thought or care for us or for our future. Gratitude becomes the single thought we substitute for these insane perceptions.

And so I became right-minded for a nanosecond in a high school auditorium and gave thanks. Driving home, I asked my daughter if she still intended to run for class president during Student Council elections later that week. She said she hadn't decided, because she didn't want to give a speech. *She has such leadership potential!* The blades of my inner helicopter whirred. I could share with her what I am learning about overcoming my fear of public speaking, how extensive preparation, rehearsal, and visualization can lessen anxiety, how…

I hope you'll excuse me while I take a moment to consult with my right mind. ☺

The Ego in Holy Spirit's Clothing

"I hate to say it but I'm not sure anyone was getting it in your class last week anyway."

I spooned coffee into the cone filter, poured the water in the coffeemaker and turned it on.

"Look, it's a matter of priorities. You have two more years

before your daughter's off to college, a stalled career to jumpstart, that short story collection to shop around, the final draft of that novel, I mean."

Through the kitchen window I watched an acrobatic squirrel race across the top of the fence as if in pursuit or under chase.

"No offense, but it's not like you're getting any younger."

In a cartoon-like tuft of grass below, our aging cat swiped at an imaginary starling.

"Not to mention the time you're putting into this blog no one's reading."

I scrambled an egg; cut up strawberries. Hummed that Sara Bareilles tune I had stuck in my head again:

I'm not gonna write you a love song
'cause you asked for it
'cause you need one

I attempted to ignore the ego, as I had once attempted to ignore the taunts of my younger brothers; nevertheless wishing for an actual body to get my hands on and throttle like I did back then, instead of this endless monologue questioning my every move with this Course I sometimes still completely forgot I had any control over at all.

All day long I had been inadvertently tuning into the ego's attempts to "reason with me" about my spiritual path until my only right-minded motivation for deciding to teach and write about *A Course in Miracles* in the first place—healing my mind— evaded me; until my clarity about which voice I had chosen to listen to—and the understanding that I could choose again— began to slip away.

"This is an independent study Course taught by Jesus or the Holy Spirit. You know what I'm saying? It's beyond words. You can't really teach it. Believing you *can* should reveal which inner teacher you've tuned into."

It was starting to sound reasonable, starting to sound a little like my right mind even.

"Look at how much time you're spending preparing for these classes. How long do you really think you can keep that up?"

I did spend a lot of time reading and listening to CDs to hone my understanding. I had been telling myself it would get easier with practice but...

"Ironic, don't you think? I mean you could actually be using that time to improve communication in your relationships. Actually have something to show for it. I don't mean to criticize or anything but it's not exactly like all this work has brought you the perfect family."

The perfect family?

I snapped out of it. Suddenly I was watching again, watching the ego do its nightclub shtick, impersonating the Holy Spirit. God, it was good. But the part of my mind that could choose was better. And so I chose again.

The ego's 24/7 rant for permanently unattainable perfection, designed to keep me mindless, wound on without my attention. Replaced by the voice from beyond this dualistic nightmare that offers the only goal I really want: the peace of God. Even when I forget I want it—as I often do—it remains forever unscathed by the ego's tale of sin and exile; forever unaffected by the instability of a world created by the thought of guilt over an impossible crime; forever free from the treadmill of seeking outside myself for the perfection of the wholeness I already eternally am.

As lesson 125, "In quiet I receive God's Word today" reminds us, however gifted a mimic the ego may be, the voice for God never stops (metaphorically) calling. When we remember we are not the ego, but the part of the mind that can choose again for the one voice we are, always calling to us from beyond the dream:

He has not waited until you return your mind to Him to give His Word to you. He has not hid Himself from you, while you wandered off a little while from Him. He does not cherish the illusions which you hold about yourself. He knows His Son, and wills that he remain as part of Him regardless of his dreams; regardless of his madness that his will is not his own.

The ego's tale of our separation from oneness is a lie. When I believed that tiny mad idea and followed the ego into a dream created to defend that illusion, my mind fused with the ego's, essentially rendering me mindless. But the memory of my true, whole self—the Holy Spirit, Jesus, our right mind—continues to reassure me I am safe. All I have to do is stop listening to the ego and there it is. So close to me I cannot fail. By watching the ego with that part of my mind, overlooking its antics and chatter and polyester suit with my inner teacher, the solidity of the dream, its figures, and its petty plot lines begins to fade.

Through practicing forgiveness I am actually beginning to experience moments of dissolution of a world designed to reinforce and preserve our phony individual, finite identities. Twice now in disagreement—first with my daughter and later with my husband—entrenched in defending the "rationality" of my position, I have completely lost track of my argument. I have forgotten my lines in the script I wrote to keep from remembering the love I am. Oddly enough, they appeared to forget their lines, too. We just stopped. Stopped and looked at each other. Stopped and looked at our feet. Stopped and looked at the four walls that seem so solid, the cat outside the window swiping at invisible enemies. Just stopped, gave it up; forgot all about it before getting on with our day.

Repeat after me (and, as always, I am talking to myself): forgiveness is simple, powerful work and it only takes one mind to do it because there is only one mind! We are only asked to watch, catch ourselves in the act of buying the ego's story—attacking or defending our own body or someone else's—and turn it over to the part of our mind that knows better, the part of our mind that remembers we are one. When and what happens next is none of our business. We do not need to understand or concern ourselves with the details of the undoing. It will come, it will be; it is already undone.

I have decided to teach and write about this Course because more than I want to retain my "special" identity I want to learn once and for always that when I choose to join with the truth I am I experience profound relief and release, even if it sometimes seems to take longer than I would like. I have decided to teach and write about this Course because it deepens my forgiveness practice. Even when the ego, increasingly threatened by my strengthening commitment, ups the ante by slipping into Holy Spirit's clothing, his plan may be foolproof, as Jesus tells us, but it is not "God-proof." I am training my proverbial ears, learning to hear and answer my underlying call for love in every attack and defense I make; learning to allow, little by little, the thought of my innocence. Each time I answer my own call for love in you, turn again toward that gentle part of my mind for help, the script shortens. One of these days I will not remember any of my lines. Only my wholeness in you.

I Love You So Much

A while back, I attended the *A Course in Miracles* conference in San Francisco representing Course organizations around the world and featuring a variety of well- and lesser-known Course speakers. As a relatively new *A Course in Miracles* student (five years versus decades) and emerging teacher, I had been working to develop my discernment skills as I listened to the many different interpretations of my chosen spiritual path. (In truth, I had been trying to figure out if the speakers were staying "true" to the Course as I saw it, a habit I had fallen into, subtly lead by the ego in Holy Spirit's clothing.) Viewpoints represented ranged from my own "purist" bent (largely informed by the teachings of Ken Wapnick) to teachers who seemed to view the Course as a self-help tool to bolster individual wellbeing, and achieve greater happiness.

As I sat listening to a speaker proceeding along the latter lines, I found myself growing more and more confused and agitated, a signal that I had once again chosen to tune into the ego's judgmental broadcast designed to keep me from remembering I can always choose which inner teacher to listen to: the ego or the Holy Spirit. In the moment I remembered I am the decision maker, not the ego; I chose again for my right mind. Almost immediately I heard the words:

"I love you so much."

Almost immediately, the ego hijacked the message and began trying to analyze and thereby distort it to a worldly, literal, special level. It was the voice of the daughter I never should have left behind in Denver calling me, in trouble maybe, perhaps in danger even.

"I love you so much."

The words came again, more clearly this time. Images of my daughter, my husband, and a handful of other loved ones currently starring in my forgiveness slide show flashed across the screen behind my eyes.

"I love you so much."

I became briefly aware of their sameness, my sameness, and the sameness of the speaker on the stage, with whom I disagreed; the sameness of friends sitting beside me and strangers seated in front and behind; the sameness of the parade of characters wending their way down Van Ness Avenue that morning as I darted out for my Americano; the sameness of the people in the North Beach restaurant last night. The particulars of their facial features and their bling, their body hardware and tattoos, their colorful costumes, blurring together like an Impressionist painting seen from a distance by the part of my mind that watches, the call of love to love instantly and forever answered.

As a young child, I spent every minute I could climbing trees in the orchards behind our house. One day, walking the tightrope of a limb, intent on snagging the shiniest of apples, I lost my balance and thudded to the ground on my back, the wind knocked out of me. For long moments I stared at a receding blackbird overhead at last absorbed into the sky. Unable to breathe, I wondered if I, too, would simply disappear into the blue void before I could draw another breath. That is how I felt that day in the lecture hall in San Francisco, poised at the edge of my dependency on the next breath that would sustain the only self I really knew.

An intense dizziness engulfed me. The room's images began to decompose into tiny paint-like blobs. The garish chandelier seemed off kilter; the shiny gold walls like the inside of a giant box of chocolates, macabre as a Toulouse Lautrec painting. My stomach turned, and turned again. My heart throbbed. I excused myself and unsteadily made my way out through the surreal corridors, up the elevator, and back into my room.

"I love you so much."

I just couldn't stomach it.

The room whirled. I wet a washcloth, drew the drapes, lay on my back on my bed in the dark, eyes covered, gripping the sides of the spinning mattress, and fighting back nausea. For the next twenty-four hours I lay there, unable to stomach my near-life brush with the oneness we are that had brought my ego to its knees. I was unable to join my friends in the activities I had planned to show off the city in which I spent my twenties, the city that had claimed a little piece of my heart. For twenty-four hours I lay on my back so distracted by the body's sensations I could not quite get my head around what had really happened in the moment of catching myself using *A Course in Miracles* to further the ego's purpose of separation, and choosing again. The moment in which I truly, fully, deeply heard perhaps for the first time the Holy Spirit's real message to our one mind:

"I love you so much."

The message from the source we never left, the message of the truth we are, the message the ego in its terror of eternal death, punishment, and damnation—of never drawing another breath—I absolutely could not stomach.

"I love you so much."

Workbook lesson 136, "Sickness is a defense against the truth," brilliantly describes the way in which we allow the ego to usurp the remembrance of the one love we are:

> Defenses are not unintentional, nor are they made without awareness. They are secret, magic wands you wave when truth appears to threaten what you would believe. They seem to be unconscious but because of the rapidity with which you choose to use them. In that second, even less, in which the choice is made, you recognize exactly what you would attempt to do, and then proceed to think that it is done.

In the moment in which I recognized with the Holy Spirit that *A Course in Miracles* needs no defenders, just as the one love we are needs no protection from illusory attack, I panicked, seduced again by the ego's fear of retribution for a crime of separation from wholeness that never happened. That unconscious, denied fear runs deep in us, but the love it masks runs deeper and will prevail despite our defenses as we continue to patiently choose again—from moment to moment—the present thought of wholeness that still thrives in our mind despite the ego's continued attacks.

> Sickness is a decision. It is not a thing that happens to you, quite unsought, which makes you weak and brings you suffering. It is a choice you make, a plan you lay, when for an instant truth arises in your own deluded mind, and all your world appears to totter and prepare to fall. Now are you sick, that truth may go away and threaten your establishments no more.

Sickness is a decision, depression is a decision, anxiety is a decision, and the underlying guilt that drives my attack on my body or your body is a decision against the truth, a decision *for* an individual identity at the expense of the only love there is. It is a decision I am learning more and more I do not want to make as I practice forgiving my investment in what cannot be, and allow the thought of love in my mind, a thought that holds myself and the you I think I see "out there" forever innocent of another (separating) point of view.

The Gratitude I Earn

Lately, I have caught myself in the act of joining in long, self-indulgent, highly enjoyable conversations with other mothers on my daughter's soccer team, equally miffed about the antics of their likewise unappreciative, insensitive spawn. I have caught myself blaming associates for failing to recognize my talents and contributions, blaming those I live with for failing to thank me for the meals, the laundry, the rides, and the sympathy I so regularly and conditionally proffer. I have caught myself in the act of offering and thereby receiving conditional gratitude, and in so doing, have severed myself from the only true gratitude that exists: gratitude for what I truly am, and for the gift of forgiveness that enables me to remember.

I went through a period in my search to reclaim what seemed missing in my life of embracing the practice of gratitude so popular in recent years: articulating a couple of things I was grateful for every day in my morning meditation; encouraging my daughter before bed each night to give thanks for the kindnesses and delights she'd experienced that day: the kid on the playground that let her go first on the ringers, the happy accident of a Golden Lab puppy encountered on a walk in the park, the taste of the tropics evoked by her favorite coconut ice cream once again available at the corner parlor, the gift of grand-parents and family friends who loved and supported her, our resilient green earth. The idea was that extending a heartfelt thank you was *more* than the right and polite thing to do; it could actually milk the universe of *more* prosperity, *more* success, *more* recognition, *more* understanding, *more* love. By counting our blessings, we could invite even more into our life, while somehow minimizing the inevitable pain of a dualistic world.

The ultimate problem? Other kids have bad days: puppies die, ice cream melts, grandparents age and sicken and can no longer visit, friends move on; our resilient green earth grows weary in its orbit of our repeated assaults in the name of human progress. Little girls who once thought you hung the moon now blame you for every obstacle encountered in their otherwise meteoric rise toward independence. And parents who once walked on water now drown in a sea of heretofore unnoticed imperfections.

The ego thought system always wants to help us devise ways to coax *more* from our illusory environment. But there is never enough to replenish the metaphoric hole we carry in our metaphoric hearts—the result of what *A Course in Miracles* calls the "tiny mad idea" of running away from the one home we share, the one and only heart that still beats in us despite our persistent denial.

However hard we try, we cannot coerce a world specifically designed by the ego to keep us seeking outside ourselves but never (permanently) finding into delivering the eternal happiness we forfeited when we believed we separated from God, and followed the ego into a projection of our guilt over that seeming rupture. Like the special love bargains we make in this world—contracts that stipulate what you must do to retain my love—our gratitude is equally conditional, based on our need for external approval and recognition for all we give. Based on a nagging sense of lack, nothing outside us can ever ultimately satisfy.

A Course in Miracles workbook lesson 197, "It can be but my gratitude I earn," describes the manipulative role gratitude plays in the ego thought system:

> You make attempts at kindness and forgiveness. Yet you turn them to attack again, unless you find external gratitude and lavish thanks. Your gifts must be received with honor, lest they be withdrawn. And so you think God's gifts are loans at best; at worst, deceptions which would cheat you of defenses, to ensure that when He strikes He will not fail to kill.

When we listen to the ego we believe that this world's God, created by the ego in its image, is equally hooked on external validation, on the habit *A Course in Miracles* calls "giving to get," a habit that at its core reflects the murderous thought of annihilating our source that drives the defense/attack cycle in which we seem hopelessly mired. The ego's God is equally stingy with his love because what passes for love in this world is ephemeral at best, and never, ever enough.

"The gratitude I earn," the unique definition of gratitude referred to in the profound spiritual psychology *A Course in Miracles,* is the true gratitude for the one love I am that—appearances to the contrary—embraces all the seeming fragments at war with themselves to prove themselves in a world that exists only in our split mind. The gratitude I earn is thankfulness for the one love I am when I remember without self-judgment to forgive what I am not: the ego's perceived need for specialness.

The gratitude I earn is my growing appreciation that no one or thing outside my mind could possibly jeopardize the peace I am despite what the body's eyes would have me believe. I earn that gratitude through the Course's radical process of forgiveness. How? By catching myself feeling unappreciated by my child, my colleague, my spouse, my friend, recognizing that the problem perceived "out there" is merely another product of my ego-identified mind, and asking for help from my right mind to see things differently.

> It does not matter if another thinks your gifts unworthy. In his mind there is a part that joins with yours in thanking you. It does not matter if your gifts seem lost and ineffectual. They are received where they are given.

Through the consistent practice of forgiveness, our one mind begins to heal. I am beginning to actually appreciate my own judgments, the red flags that remind me I have once again forfeited happiness by believing in an illusion of unfair treatment. But it is all in my mind and I can and must choose again. Recognizing my true identity in the person I want to blame for overlooking all I have given, eventually teaches me to awaken from this nightmare of specialness and separation I have chosen over perfect unity. And so I offer thanks today for once again reclaiming my innocence—growing a little more conscious, a little bit closer to awakening—by changing my mind about you.

The Real Secret

My daughter snarled at me; the computer locked up mid-download, and locked again. I lost two new files; the muffins burned; I had writer's block; the client and the dentist did not return my phone calls; I stubbed my toe; it wouldn't stop raining. My daughter headed out again and I was worried; my daughter and her entourage returned and ransacked the kitchen; my husband misunderstood me again; it wouldn't stop raining. My eyes itched with pollen; the computer crashed; I was starting to wheeze, and the cat did its hairball thing on the rug. The pizza delivery never made it. Another client put off the project again; a microburst of hail nuked my basil. I couldn't fall asleep; I couldn't seem to wake up; the chocolate I ate to mitigate my troubles tasted off; my daughter snarled at me...

For days I witnessed my discomfort with every little curve life threw me, stuck in the director's chair at the center of my split mind somehow unable to make the necessary choice against the ego thought system that would enable the resurgence of inner peace. A choice that would automatically allow me to hear the only instructions my right mind had truly ever uttered: "It never happened." It, meaning the impossible separation from our source, the choice for individuality and dueling interests over perfect oneness the ego continues to champion. The consequences of which the ego continues to insist we blame on a constant barrage of outside assaults designed to keep us from recognizing our underlying guilt over an impossible crime; to keep us from recognizing we have a mind that chose this in the first place and can always make a better choice.

The movie *The Secret* has generated a lot of buzz over the last few years. Although based on "the law of attraction"—the New Age belief that focusing on positive thoughts while avoiding negative attracts more positive—it also sounds suspiciously retro. Just listen to the lyrics of the 1940s Perry Como tune, the one my Aunt Margaret used to play while she twirled me around the room:

You gotta accentuate the positive
Eliminate the negative an' latch on to the affirmative
Don't mess with Mister In Between

The song resonates as a kind of anthem for "The Greatest Generation." It espouses putting a brave mask on the horrors of a world on the brink of annihilation. Like the principles advocated by the law of attraction, it may have helped a generation survive and perhaps even flourish for a while but did little to deliver them from the "evils" of the ego thought system we all share. This is a thought system designed at best to offer temporary relief and distraction from the scenario we call a life that always ends the same way regardless of the good stuff we may have accumulated between birth and death.

Other wars followed and The Greatest Generation watched as its silent majority values appeared to detonate under the assaults of ungrateful children hell-bent on overturning an establishment perceived as stunting their adventures in civil disobedience and higher consciousness. All these years later, *The Secret* has fallen short of its promise as it inevitably must. Wars continue to rage. Teenagers continue to protest the ill-conceived institutions their elders have crafted before moving on to create their own. The planet continues to sicken at its keepers' hands. And we're still avoiding messing with "Mister In Between," the neutral decision maker in our mind *A Course in Miracles'* forgiveness practice teaches us can always choose again for the permanent, positive outcome of the whole, eternal love we are (and in truth have never left).

We're afraid to choose for love because it's all mixed up in our wrong mind with the impossible "sin" of separation and the lingering desire to experience individuality. The real secret of eternal peace requires us to recognize that we don't want to heal our mind, we don't want to take responsibility for our judgments and belief in unfair treatment, and we certainly don't want to turn our perceptual errors over to an inner teacher that offers a better way. There's nothing sexy about the real secret that simply requires us to begin watching how we allow the most minor irritations to derail our day; to begin to recognize the murderous foundation of the ego thought system responsible for every seeming problem "out there," from allergies, technological diffi-culties, and wayward pets to world war, ethnic cleansing, tornadoes, and global warming.

The real secret to the universe ultimately requires us to entertain the shocking idea that there is no universe, only a complex barrage of dream images, conjured as if by Mickey Mouse as Merlin in the classic Disney cartoon *Fantasia*, to reinforce and preserve a seemingly unique identity. The real secret requires me to recognize my physical and psychological body exists only in the one mind dreaming its dreamy dream of exile from perfect wholeness.

We cannot begin to recognize there is nothing "out there" until we begin to honestly look at the ugliness of the infinite, ingenious disguises the ego-identified mind has designed to keep us defending ourselves from love by fighting non-existent battles. We cannot begin to recognize the ego's ill intentions if we spend all our time trying to cover them over, dress them up, emphasize the positive, latch on to the affirmative, and refuse to mess with Mister In Between.

We must learn to embrace the real secret of the universe: that it does not exist. We imagined it because we wanted to experience autonomy even if it meant forfeiting eternal happiness. We attempt to hide the enormous guilt we feel over our choice to believe in that "tiny mad idea" by embracing techniques for solving problems and manifesting solutions in a world specifically designed to keep us playing "out there:" a world invented to prevent us from ever returning to the part of our mind that can choose again for the only real solution; remembering the love we never left.

Continually focusing on the positive and denying the negative may help us achieve short-term goals, but it prevents us from ever accessing our magnificence by choosing again for our right mind that sees only common interests. It is a "defense against the truth," another tool the ego uses to keep the awareness of love's eternal, indivisible presence from resurfacing in our mind. We must consistently watch how easily and regularly we allow everything seemingly "out there" to ransack our peace before we can turn to our inner teacher for help. When we choose to stop denying the misery of the ego thought system, take back responsibility for our large and small projections, and turn them over to the part of our mind that knows better, we enable the only real attraction alive in our one mind: the attraction of love for the love it has always been and always will be.

Be Careful "Out There"

Sitting in a class offered by the School of Reason for teachers and aspiring teachers of *A Course in Miracles*, I had a revelatory experience that still reverberates in my head. As I listened to a fellow student reading from workbook lesson 199, "I am not a body. I am free," her voice transformed, grew vast, echoing a beauty beyond words. I could almost hear every voice ever raised in this seeming world united in its eternal breadth. It enveloped me, transporting me far beyond the confines of the body the ego made to keep its message from ever resurfacing in my mind. It gently placed me at the threshold of true awareness discussed in Chapter 19, "The Lifting of the Veil," where we embrace once and for always the collective nature of our return to the truth we never really left.

Together we will disappear into the Presence beyond the veil, not to be lost but found, not to be seen but known.

For a moment listening to the sound of a voice beyond all voices—the call of love to the love we are and have never left—I embraced complete wholeness. I accepted with enthusiasm, and even excitement, the dissolution of this seemingly separate identity the ego would have me defend to the death. My apparently split mind healed. I no longer desired to be seen, only known. I entered our oneness unfettered by the petty, tortured details of the ego's impossible dream.

"What veil?" The ego asked as I drove home.

I paid it no mind. I was one with my fellow students and teachers in the School of Reason, one with passengers in the cars whizzing by, one with an old man bending to water a plot of tomatoes, a college student zigzagging home on his bike, the acrobatic squirrel racing up the trunk of a cottonwood as if ascending a ladder to truth.

At home, I discovered my daughter had gone out again without my permission, leaving a sink full of dishes. My husband had neglected to take out the trash or recycling or refrigerate the remains of the dinner I had left him, and a client had not returned my email about our conference call the next morning.

The ego clicked its tongue and rolled its eyes.

I paid it no mind. I climbed the stairs and went to bed, dreaming of standing at the edge of an infinite swimming pool holding hands with everyone that had ever seemed to live: raising our voices in harmonious song like the animated Whos in *The Grinch Who Stole Christmas*, at peace with the disappearance of material gifts.

The next day I awoke with a pinched nerve in my neck, one hell of a craving for sugar, and the ego nestled on my shoulder batting its eyelids like the Anti-Jiminy Cricket.

"We need to talk," it said.

Searing nerve pain skated around my skull, seemingly circumventing access to my right mind. I had been here before. My experiences with what *A Course in Miracles* refers to as the holy instant—a moment of complete communion with our source, the result of returning our illusions to our one mind and choosing again for truth—are almost always followed by the *ego's backlash*. Sometimes it impersonates a neglected child, parent, or spouse, apparently guilt-tripping me. Sometimes it morphs into a cross-examining attorney. Sometimes it enters the "healing" professions coaxing me to pay more attention to the physical/psychological symptoms it has rallied to its defense. No matter its chosen role, the purpose of its drama never wavers. It will do or say anything to seduce me back into the fold, to make me forget I have a mind that is learning it wants to choose again.

I have tried many times to ignore the ego but am finally realizing that trying to ignore it is a little like trying to ignore a verbally gifted teenage girl hell-bent on making her point. I have learned through experience that turning to face the teenager and the ego—allowing them to spew their faulty rhetoric, feel truly seen and heard—sometimes offers the most effective long-term strategy to restoring peace of mind.

And so I went downstairs, put on a pot of coffee, toasted a couple frozen waffles, and sat down once more to listen with our inner teacher to the oxymoron of the ego's logic, trusting it would once again talk itself out, allowing me to get on with my forgiveness opportunities.

Ego: That kid of yours is a regular pain in the neck.

Me: ☺

Ego: So you're just going to ignore those dishes?

Me: It's not like they're mine.

Ego: My point exactly. Isn't there a little parental conversation someone needs to be having with you know who?

Me: You said we needed to *talk*?

Ego: Fine. Communication is key, I always say. If people would just communicate honestly there'd be a lot less suffering in this world.

Me: And we know you are all about ending human suffering.

Ego: Sarcastic; I've always admired that in you.

Me: Thanks. So what's on your mind?

Ego: What mind?

Me: Funny.

Ego: Thanks. Okay, it's not like I mind you neglecting *me*. But when you start neglecting your daughter, your husband, your work, your house plants.

Me: My house plants?

Ego: May I venture to add your health?

Me: What? Are you sure we're not talking about someone else feeling neglected?

Ego: You're a laugh a minute this morning. I mean to sit around that classroom yawning and scratching yourselves while reading about how you're not bodies. Hallucinating about disappearing into some kind of primordial broth.

Me: Eavesdropping on my dreams again I see.

Ego: Honey, I am your dreams if you know what I'm saying.

Me: Only too well.

Ego: Could you even hear your own stomach grumbling last night?

Me: What stomach?

Ego: You kill me, you really do. Anyway, where was I—oh yeah, disappearing into some kind of primordial broth like that's a *good* thing? And all this talk about voices, I mean, they have names for people like you.

Me: And places to put them if I'm not mistaken.

Ego: *Exactly.*

Me: So you think I might be having some kind of psychotic break?

Ego: In your case, who knows? You've always been a little...what did your mother used to call it—high strung? Nothing clinical, exactly, a tad bipolar maybe. Let's just say a little *different.* (Wink, wink.)

Me: It's all in the genes.

Ego: I couldn't have said it better myself. Then again there could be more to that pinched nerve than meets the eye.

Me: What eye?

Ego: You're killing me, I mean it.

Me: More than your fear of disappearing into the primordial broth?

Ego: *You're* a primordial broth.

Me: Can I quote you on that?

Ego: I'm just saying you might want to get that neck of yours checked out. Maybe it's a pinched nerve. Or maybe it's—I don't know.

Me: A brain tumor?

Ego: Your words, not mine.

Me: OK, Woody Allen, so you sure you're not feeling the teeniest little bit threatened by this Course?

Ego: *Excuse* me? Have we even met? What the hell would I have to be threatened about? *You're* the one on the verge of jumping into a swimming pool with a bunch of cartoon characters because you think there's no body.

Me: *Fah who for-aze!*

Dah who dor-aze!

(I hummed.)

Ego: Look, you want to get diabetes, just keep pounding those waffles.

Me: As enjoyable as this has been I really do need to get some work done this morning. Deadlines, and all that.

Ego: You have no idea how much I *love* to hear you say that word.

Me: You'd be surprised. Any parting words of advice?

Ego: Step *away* from the waffles. You can do it—just say no.

Me: I love it when you talk all Nancy Reagan to me.

Ego: Always looking out for your best interests.

Me: Jeez, you make me feel so special.

Ego: It's a gift.

Me: Right. Anything else?

Ego: Lay down the law with that husband and kid of yours before it's too late. Tough love, you know what I'm saying?

Me: Only too well.

Ego: And just one more thing.

Me: Sure.

Ego: Be careful out there.

You had to love it. Well; maybe not so much anymore.

I carried my dishes to the sink, carefully washed them and slipped them into the drainer without disturbing my daughter's congealing, listing tower of debris. We could talk when she woke up, no pun intended.

I filled an ice pack for my neck and headed back to my

computer to get on with my writing.

You *Can* Go Home Again

We know nothing. You are now up to speed.
Steve Martin as Inspector Clouseau, *Pink Panther 2*

In the set I constructed in which to act out my coming of age, there are many flags and many fences. Stone walls that once protected revolutionary freedom fighters from the Red Coats continue to dissect weed-choked territory, proclaiming old victories and bemoaning old slaughters. Signs boast first roads, Benedict Arnold's sneaky ways, and the random honor of our nation's founder, George Washington, bunking down on plank floors for the night. Ranch and modular homes sporting design elements swiped from the few majestic colonials that prevail from those days of brazen independence crowd lime-tinted hillsides. But our forefathers' dreams of perennial liberty notwithstanding, houses and bodies still sicken and die despite their inhabitants' best efforts.

I have just returned from visiting my family on the Hudson River, forty plus miles north of New York City. Normally we descend on my parents' cabin hugging the Canadian woods at the state's northern boundary but a combination of exorbitant airfares and erratic summer work schedules this year converged to bring us all together at my brother's home, the remodeled ranch house I grew up in. I had not spent time in this revolutionary war town in decades and had ample leisure to reflect on both a nation's impulse to free itself from Mother England's tyranny and my own reenactment of that universal urge.

My father still refers to my initial move to California in my early twenties as "when you took off," and often measures family events before and after in relationship to that phrase. That I bolted thirty years ago means little; that I was the only one of our tribe to do so means a lot less than it used to—to me at least.

Maybe because I now understand that despite the superficial differences that once loomed in my adolescent brain, the only real separation that could possibly divide us never occurred. Although, like all of us here dreaming of exile, we continue to reinforce its consequences in our split mind.

A Course in Miracles calls the relationships we most cherish and abhor—those with our parents, children, siblings, spouses, romantic and business partners—the alliances the ego thought system invented to reinforce and protect a rift from our source that never happened—"special relationships." They are projected symbols of the buried guilt in our one mind over that seeming attack on our singular source. On the level of form in which we operate, however—the world that seems so solid and menacing—they are bargains we make with others to get our (largely unspoken) needs met. If you will meet my need to feel recognized, accepted, celebrated, revered, I will reciprocate. But no amount of recognition, acceptance, celebration, or reverence can permanently fill the gaping hole we carry in our mind. The haunting emptiness we experience as a result of the false belief that we have forfeited the one, whole, eternal, non-specific love we are.

The ego uses our special relationships to relieve our repressed guilt and prove its mantra of "seek but do not find." Like our own bodies, our closest relationships provide only fleeting pleasure. In them we unconsciously reenact the attack-defense cycle at the core of the ego thought system. We believe we attacked God by our choice to separate, and now must defend ourselves from his retribution. We do that by projecting the buried guilt in our mind onto others in a pathetic effort to prove our own innocence. We believe that those we include in our orbit—our kin, our next-door neighbors, those who share and validate our political affiliations, our preferences, and values over those of the "outsiders"—protect and support us. They shore us up in tough times and help us deal with the toll time

93

takes on our bodies and belongings. But nothing can ultimately protect and support us in a world specifically designed to prove that the "sin" of independence actually occurred and deserves the final punishment of death all humans face.

It's all smoke and mirrors designed to keep us from ever returning to the part of our mind that decided to side with the ego in the first place but can just as easily choose again for the part of our mind that remembers what we are. There is only one possible relationship—our relationship with the memory of truth/love in our one mind. Geared toward a prevailing Western culture, *A Course in Miracles* uses the Holy Spirit or Jesus to reflect that memory but they are merely symbolic of a mind healed of the original belief in divided love and loyalty. The unique forgiveness the Course offers galvanizes our relationships to heal that fissure. Learning to overlook our mistaken perception of reenacted separate interests in our special relationships allows us to begin to experience the one, eternal love we have buried in our one, eternal mind. When we choose to stop listening to the ego's twenty-four-hour soap opera of sin, guilt, and fear, we can (metaphorically) hear clearly the call of the love we never left. Restored to our right mind, we then come from a loving, gentle, accepting, unconditional place in our interactions with others without any effort to fix behavior.

The beauty of *A Course in Miracles* is the radical forgiveness practice it offers us to get back to our right mind, the ingenious way it teaches us to use our illusions to undo them. The first step requires us to observe how much we want to control and attack others. Everyone does this and there's no need to beat ourselves up about it. It's crazy to judge ourselves for doing what the ego designed bodies to do. Instead, we must observe our denied impulses to attack and the unhappiness they cause us with our inner teacher to be motivated to accept a better way. We must learn to bring ourselves up to speed by admitting we know nothing and turning instead to the part of our mind that retains the knowledge of everything.

A Course in Miracles is not teaching us to be more loving. Trying to fix an illusion does not work. Instead, it teaches us to allow the undoing of a thought system based on a lie that keeps us from experiencing the love we already are. It teaches us to allow the removal of the blocks the ego mind has placed to keep the awareness of that love from resurfacing in our mind. It teaches us to catch ourselves holding our special relationships responsible for our peace; to recognize the problem and its solution is not rooted in a place "out there" but in our one mind, and to ask our inner teacher to see things differently. When we choose in this way to remember our true nature, we experience complete, eternal, unalterable peace, and begin to reflect it more in our relationships.

It only takes one mind to heal. I am married to a man who has no interest in *A Course in Miracles*. He would sooner eat glass than crack open that big blue book. We are extremely different personalities and so have naturally experienced conflict. I have been practicing the Course for five years and while we still have completely different personalities, our relationship appears to have become much more peaceful. I say *appears* because the Course does not focus on changing external behavior, only on changing our mind. By committing to practicing forgiveness every time a conflict arises in my relationship with my husband and teenage daughter, I am beginning to experience elongated moments of deep relief and release from the burden of the ego thought system of competing interests.

There are now times in mid disagreement when I completely forget my investment in my argument and he seems to do the same thing, as if we can no longer remember the script we wrote to keep us at odds. Only common interests prevail. When he is upset, I have begun to truly recognize it as my upset, the upset we all share over the impossible belief that we destroyed love. The compassion I am developing for him is my compassion for

95

myself. The fear of love I witness in him is my own. Practicing forgiveness, remembering there is only one mind on ego and turning my error over to our inner teacher for gentle correction, the guilt in my mind lifts and I am greatly relieved of its exhausting responsibility. I am enormously grateful to my husband and daughter for the healing of my mind.

Practicing forgiveness in my marriage and as a parent has given my life new meaning—in truth, the only meaning it could ever have. I now recognize that lasting happiness is not of this world, but there is a love beyond that can never fail me. I awaken to that love by practicing forgiveness, taking my projections back to my mind and choosing again. The Course gives us the tools to do that.

It hurts to begin to look at how much we want to hold someone or something "out there" responsible for our lack of peace. But we don't have to (and in truth, cannot) do it alone. We must call on the inner teacher in our mind. If it helps to imagine Jesus taking your hand, do it; he will grasp it. If it helps to hear his voice, he will speak to you. He will meet us where we think we are until our fear subsides enough to recognize that the hand and the voice are in truth our husbands' and daughters' and parents' and bosses'; our brothers' and sisters' and lovers' and enemies.' Our special relationships save us when we remember to practice forgiveness. We can go home again. We return to our one and only true home and freedom together. I find my innocence and liberation at last in you.

A Day in the Life of the Decision Maker

A Course in Miracles addresses the part of our mind that chose to side with the ego's hallucination of separation from our source but can choose again for the part of our mind that knows it is only a dream. Dr. Kenneth Wapnick adopted the term decision maker from a reference in the Course's *Teachers' Manual* to describe that chooser in our mind. The concept has helped me enormously in practicing the Course's unique form of forgiveness. Learning to rest in the part of our mind that can observe and choose, rather than blindly buying the ego's sob story of sin, guilt, and fear, begins to allow the undoing of the ego thought system, eventually enabling us to awaken from a dualistic dream to the unity of the love we are.

When we pay attention, we begin to see that we can choose all day long between the ego and the Holy Spirit, the voice for separation and fear and the voice for love. *A Course in Miracles* is not asking us to demonstrate how kind and holy we are but to begin to notice how we choose to reinforce the mistaken notion of duality by attacking and defending against a perennial cast of imaginary enemies, how easily we succumb to the ego's disturbed reasoning. However appealing the ego's tale of separate interests designed to bolster the seeming reality of our unique identities, we will never find permanent happiness following the ego. We must ask for help from the part of our mind that remembers certain, unalterable peace to see things differently. The Course calls this process of overlooking the absolute impossibility of separate interests with our right mind, forgiveness. When we choose to activate this part of our mind we automatically come from a tolerant, gentle, loving place in our relationships. Here's how it works in a typical day:

6 a.m.

Wolf down supplements. Chase with healthy breakfast of sliced fruit and yogurt to compensate for less than temperate ingestion of steak, chocolate mousse, and key lime pie the night before: a sacrifice made to accommodate my husband's manly food preferences; a Father's Day dinner my daughter and I had planned, shopped for, and even cooked together, chatting happily away about the encouraging possibility of her completing the tasks attached to her side of our embryonic buying-your-first-car negotiations (not unlike Jane Wyatt and I can't remember the actress's name in the old *Father Knows Best* sitcom: the teenage daughter the father called "Kitten." No one ever called me Kitten. It can still tick me off if I let it. I choose for my right mind instead).

6:45 a.m.

In my office, eyes closed, communing with my right mind as I do every morning, asking for guidance in approaching my forgiveness curriculum for the day. Usual mental forgiveness slide show replaced by prayers of thanks for remarkable evening last night. A feeling of genuine gratitude for my husband's parenting strengths—generosity, engagement, humor, empathy—washes over me. My daughter had made a salad, set the table without my asking, and put on a CD she had burned— her interpretation of what our favorite songs might be had we been born thirty-five years later as her peer. We'd sat outside in a lush garden nourished by torrential rains, our tomatoes stretching toward the last of the day's welcome sunlight. Listening to someone born yesterday who is probably texting even as I speak perform a decent rendition of *Summer Breeze*, my appreciation for the miracle of it all growing *"like the jasmine in my mind."* My husband and daughter slipped sibling-like into their own little cocoon as they are apt to do, flipping through old photos of their childhood together, poring over *Consumer Report* printouts of potential vehicles. Somehow, admiration for their adorable similarities replaced my all too frequent nagging feelings of exclusion.

7:30 a.m.

Dealing with emails and writing project even though it is Saturday. No rest for the freelancer, I always say. That would be my ego, of course, I, the decision maker, knew that. But you still have to deal with form; things called deadlines, even though it is one of my wrong mind's favorite words. There are still things here in form to cross off the perennial "To Do" list; the trick is to not take it all so seriously. Anyway, once I get this out of the way and throw in some laundry I'm on to a workout on the elliptical downstairs, hoping to finish Ken Wapnick's CD "Return of the Repressed." Again. Can't hear about the ego's boomerang ways too many times I always say. That would be my right mind. I hope.

9 a.m.

Front doorbell rings. A tall, young, stressed-out guy from the next door landscaping project is sorry to report he backed his gigantic flat bed truck into my relatively petite Subaru Outback while trying to park with unfortunate results. I follow him down the sidewalk to observe the front of my car strewn across the pavement like a disassembled robot. He waits in the doorway while I take down his insurance information, congratulating myself on my failure to listen to the ego's blather about how I need this today like I need a hole in the head. I even feel sorry for the guy. It's been raining all week; he's behind on this and all the other jobs he oversees. I sit with him on the stoop nodding like a therapist, gathering information before heading back in to call my insurance company.

9:20 a.m.

Dial insurance company weekend phone service number and calmly follow multiple computer-generated voice prompts before initial intake person records information, assigns a claim number, and transfers me to a claims person who cordially invites me to repeat the story all over again. Continue to congratulate myself on not getting triggered over the type of random event that could have induced apoplectic state in pre-Course, type-A personality Susan. Acutely aware of pre-Course Susan's ego-driven impulse to perceive herself unfairly treated, bemoan the derailment of her plans for the day, engage in internal monologue on the dangers of suffering fools, and begin trying to analyze why on earth she would have created something like this in the first place.

9:35 a.m.

Claims lady explains she will need to hang up and call the

tall, young, stressed-out landscape guy to take a report, call his adjuster, and get back to me in a couple days about what to do next, even though we are both covered by the same insurance company. I calmly explain this makes no sense since tall, young, stressed-out landscape guy is working next door and I can easily carry the phone out and let her talk to him right now. She repeats what she needs to do and how she will get back to me in a couple of days. (She has this great recorded-sounding voice; my ego wonders if they practice that.) I, the decision maker, repeat my alternative. (Not sure how long our dueling instant replay continues but do recall ego wondering if we may have slipped into one of Dante's heretofore unspecified circles of hell.)

Finally manage to explain I am going out of town Wednesday and need to take my car in before I leave. My plan will greatly expedite the process. Insurance lady finally agrees to allow me to put tall, young, stressed-out landscape guy on the phone while I continue to marvel over how—the ego's wisecracks notwithstanding—I, the decision maker, have not taken any of this personally nor forfeited my peace of mind—a huge shift from pre-Course Susan's typical meltdowns.

10:00 a.m.

Walking to rental car place rather than waiting an hour for their driver to come pick me up. It begins to rain. Again. I do not have an umbrella. It never rains in the morning in Denver. Not this hard anyway. I do not take it personally.

11:30 a.m.

Abbreviated workout downstairs to Ken Wapnick's CD. Something about the love hidden beneath the ego's attacks I have understood before but suddenly cannot seem to wrap my proverbial head around. My daughter needs a ride to the mall to check on her hours for the second of two jobs she has landed but so far this summer never actually been scheduled to work. She keeps popping her head around the stairs at me. The ego starts muttering something about ungrateful, self-centered spawn. I, the decision maker, choose to listen to the part of my mind that does not take it seriously. I give up on my workout and go take a quick shower.

1 p.m.

My daughter busts out of the clothing store shaking her head. The mall is largely empty; the generation-next manager cannot put her on for a shift until after we return from visiting family next week. She did not take the summer school swimming class she could have to get the credits she needs over with or arrange for volunteer work to get a jump on her extensive community service requirements. So far her summer schedule resembles that of a reality TV show about the rich and spoiled minus the cash—rising midday to trash the kitchen, catching up on recorded TV programs, and joining friends for a swim before heading out for the evening. She does not yet drive, although many of her friends do. I supply the rest of the rides and oscillate between watching myself resenting the chauffer services I provide and fretting over the dangers of rides supplied by her inexperienced friends.

I notice resentment rising up again in me, my intense attraction to the belief that my teenager—all teenagers, really—is the problem. I have never really liked teenagers, not even when I was one. I recognize these thoughts as my ego's, and ask for help in looking at my perception. I am reminded there is only one problem, my belief in separation, and only one solution, overlooking with my inner teacher what cannot be. I suddenly realize my daughter may feel just as disappointed as I do, maybe even a little rejected by the summer's turn of events. She is only sixteen after all. I loop my arm around her. "Kitten," I say. "What?" she says, and pulls away. Over lunch we discuss other possible ways for her to earn money toward that car.

3 p.m.

Finish the writing project earlier interrupted by tall, young, stressed-out landscape guy slamming into my vehicle. Uncharacteristic rain has once again washed out plans for a picnic along the Platte with friends who live downtown. My husband and I agree to meet them at their place before heading on to an early theatre engagement. My daughter asks if she can have a girlfriend over while we are gone. The rain has stopped and they plan to ride their bikes and hang out in the park, maybe take a hot tub. We normally do not allow visitors while we're gone but it will be just the two of them, she reassures me, outside most of the time.

6:30 p.m.

Enjoying an indoor picnic and panoramic view of the front-range and lower downtown Denver at friends' loft. Our daughter sends my husband a text message. She and a couple of girlfriends are meeting in the park. When I ask if he reminded her they cannot be inside he waves me away, vague and unconcerned about the details. We are late for the theatre and pile into his car. They know they cannot hang out inside with us gone, I repeat softly. Of his many parenting strengths, consistency is conspicuously missing. He is not concerned. I ignore a bad feeling about this. After all, she knows the rules. I can't tell for sure who is talking at the moment. I sit in a director's chair staring down my right and wrong mind—the truth in me and its "evil" twin—confused and seemingly unable to choose.

9 p.m.

Home from the theatre obviously earlier than expected to find my daughter's friend sitting on the couch with a boy, lights out, my daughter upstairs in her room with another boy, our cardboard, life-size statue of Obama (a family fixture since last year's Democratic National Convention in Denver) moved from the basement to the stairs, as if standing sentry. Sadly, our President appears to have been slacking off on the job. Luckily pre-Course Susan is back! What was that F word again, she asks?

The ego always speaks first and it has a mouthful to share although I, the decision maker, have the presence of mind not to repeat it out loud, vaguely aware I am not in my right mind. Still,

I call my daughter aside to ask her which part of our rules about not having boys in the house she does not understand. She seizes the offensive. They weren't doing anything for God's sake; they're just friends; they were only there for a few minutes because it started raining, etc.

She does not look like a projection. I recognize I cannot respond without anger. Everyone needs to go home, I explain. We'll talk in the morning. The kids leave. My husband is already lying low in his downstairs office glued to the computer screen. There is nothing the ego can say I will not regret. Pre-Course Susan could not have known this. At least I, the decision maker, have that to cling to. I go to bed, begging for help from my right mind to *want* to choose again.

6 a.m.

Wolf down supplements and healthy breakfast of fruit and cereal, marveling over failure to go ballistic the night before. Head to office to commune, eyes closed, with my right mind. Daughter and husband's faces flash through my forgiveness slide show. I choose again for the voice of reason, knowing from experience it will bring me peace. I open my eyes and jot down a list of rules to review with my daughter when she wakes up, smiling at the metaphor. The phone rings. The insurance company has not yet approved my rental car. Which credit card did I want to put that on? ☺

A Course in Miracles Survivor

At times it felt like a reality TV program entitled *A Course in Miracles Survivor*. There were nine of us students on the island to start, plus two facilitators, long-time Course teachers Lyn Corona and Chris Dixon. We joked that the twelfth member was Jesus/Holy Spirit/our right mind, and in truth could feel an awakened presence strengthening in us as we did the hard work of looking at the ingenious hurdles our belief in the ego thought system threw our way, fortified by the lifelong work of Ken

Wapnick, founder of the *Foundation for A Course in Miracles*.

Together, we had embraced the first two-year curriculum offered by the School of Reason (SOR) for teachers and aspiring teachers of *A Course in Miracles*, a program designed to apply Course wisdom in our daily lives, while moving deeply into portions of the Course and related materials most concerned with recognizing and undoing the ego thought system. We "lost" three students along the way. One realized it was not the right time for her; another, a long-time student of both Buddhism and the Course, eventually identified the former as his chosen path. The third discovered he had many more spiritual roads to travel on his way home. The Course does not bill itself as the only return to truth. We bid them a fond farewell, knowing we would meet again in wholeness at the end of the road.

Last week, we "survivors" assembled to celebrate the completion of the beginning of the journey without distance the Course refers to, a metaphorical voyage of awakening from a dualistic dream of separate interests to unity. The Course calls our everyday experience in the dream—our interactions with others, the events and situations that provoke us to attack or defend—our curriculum. It teaches us to use these very challenges to undo our belief in and attraction to individual interests. We are all "teachers of God" when we demonstrate this kind of forgiveness. But we had intentionally taken it a step further by committing to join in our learning and healing, and to share our experience with others.

We spent our first semester studying and listening to Ken Wapnick's comments on the "What It Says" portion of the Preface and other CDs, examining the early text chapters, and creating and presenting our own diagrams and interpretations of the two thought systems and the creation myth upon which the Course's teaching relies. Our resistance to "getting it" was strong. The last thing the ego wants us to do is examine the dynamic of sin/guilt/fear it set in motion when it convinced us to believe in the "tiny, mad, idea" of separation from our source. Some of us reported falling asleep during study. Some became visibly confused in class. Some grew defensive. There were times when I experienced all of these states, along with an overwhelming terror of presenting. On many occasions, I compared myself unfavorably to other students. On others, feelings of unbridled competition reared their ugly heads. I learned to recognize them for what they were—defenses against the truth—and do it anyway.

In between classes I continued to watch my attraction to holding my husband and daughter (what the Course calls our "special relationships") responsible for my loss of (or return to) peace. Asking—more often pleading—to recognize my projected guilt over an impossible rift and choose again for the part of my mind that remembers our invulnerability.

In our second semester, we began preparing and presenting portions of the text and teaching a workbook class for new ACIM students. I begged for help with my fear, did it anyway, and discovered just how heavily supported we really are. "I am so close to you we cannot fail," Jesus tells us in the introduction to Part II of the workbook, and reminds us again and again throughout the material. But I had never really heard those words, or allowed the deep comfort they offered in answer to my deep longing, until I started to teach and finally understood that teaching and learning really are exactly the same. I found through presenting to my colleagues and later to new students not only a bridge across my own terror of public speaking but a bridge over the troubled waters of this world back to my right mind. Over time, feelings of competition and comparison, the ego's story of individual specialness began to weaken. And I began to notice not only the way the ego retaliated following my exploration/presentation on a particular workbook lesson or text section, but the way in which I created specific lessons in my life to strengthen my forgiveness practice.

Over our break last summer for example, assigned the *Song of Prayer* and *Psychotherapy* pamphlets and complementary materials on the Course's teachings around healing, a routine CT-scan discovered a "lesion" on my liver identified months later in a second scan as a harmless birthmark. The fear that gripped me during that interval allowed me to deeply delve into my investment in this body/identity and fully experience just how attracted I am to this world of separation from our source and this persona my mind created to keep me here. I realized how much I wanted to make the original error of separation real, and began to learn to truly forgive my investment in specialness. I embraced the truth that I will die, everyone I love will die; that is what bodies do, and began to allow the idea that I am something beyond all this, something vast and whole, impersonal, unalterable, and steadily loving; something I really want to remember. I don't have to wait to die to understand this; I can awaken to it now, moment by moment, as I practice with my right mind overlooking what never was, as I begin to really experience that "nothing real can be threatened."

During the first class of our last semester, we set the following intention for the final leg of our journey together in the SOR: "Our scattered goals blend into one intent: we want the peace of God!" Then we embarked on a detailed investigation of the Course sections on The Laws of Chaos and The Obstacles to Peace. We spent so much time on the latter that it began to feel like the movie *Groundhog Day*. For one reason or another I kept being asked to present on the subsection involving The Attraction of Pain, and the illuminating culmination: The Lifting of the Veil. During my inquiry of the former I fractured my hip, and saw exactly how I used physical pain to separate from others and reinforce the ego's sob story of unfair treatment. I was able to see and release that idea almost instantaneously, and found, to my astonishment, that my husband and daughter appeared loving and helpful during a long recovery that would have launched pre-Course Susan into a smashing meltdown.

While studying The Lifting of the Veil, in which Jesus explains the collective nature of our return to wholeness, I also began to see how much I want to exclude others from my journey home. I looked closely at the constant ego temptation to congratulate myself on my Course understanding versus what my mind on ego considered the mistaken interpretations of Course students and teachers who viewed ACIM as a kind of self-help, law-of-attracting, manifesting-your-destiny tool. I learned to catch the ego attempting to hijack the journey, and ask for help in remembering the singular nature of the mind. Despite appearances in the world of perception, there is still only one split mind that chooses between the ego's illusion and the Holy Spirit's memory of truth, one split mind in need of healing. It is not in my best interests to use the Course to separate if I want the peace of God. I cannot get home without taking my illusion back to its origin.

Practicing forgiving my belief that my husband and daughter could disturb my peace eventually expanded to include everyone and everything seemingly "out there." Not always I am sorry to report. Not even most of the time. But more and more. I wanted the peace of God, after all, and had committed to my colleagues to find it: colleagues who also found themselves staring down their own particular demons in their particular curriculum, learning to identify the one problem, and apply the one solution. At some point, bolstered by the loving, forgiving support of comrades equally dedicated to waking up, for the first time, my desire to return to God outweighed my desire to hide in the illusion, and I began to notice an increased awareness of the choice available in each moment. I could no longer get away with choosing the ego for very long. It hurt too much, and besides I had begun to actually believe in the idea that we return together or not at all.

And so we survivors go on forgiving. We did not want to use

the term graduation because the real school, like everything else in our dream of exile from the one love we truly are, exists only in our one mind, along with the one teacher we carry with us and can always turn to for clarity. Nevertheless, joining together in form to honor our mutual dedication, reflect on our journey to date, and re-strengthen our commitment feels right.

As we met last week, Lyn and Chris transformed a corner of Lyn's apartment building penthouse into an elegant dining oasis complete with crisp linens, fine crystal and cutlery, and clusters of lilies. Flowers symbolic of the peace always available to us when we turn away from the ego's endless boasts and gripes and meet in stillness with our inner teacher to smile gently at our error and allow our truth. To my mighty companions in forgiveness in the SOR, the survivors and those who decided to heal their minds elsewhere, and to everyone everywhere longing for unity, I raise a toast of appreciation and a hand to grasp. We return together regardless of how the details of our maps home vary. Thank you again for your growing willingness to open your eyes despite your fear, to take our teacher's hand, and to continue to find our innocence together.

Holy Spirit AWOL

Here is the fear of God most plainly seen. For love is treacherous to those who fear, since fear and hate can never be apart. No one who hates but is afraid of love, and therefore must he be afraid of God. Certain it is he knows not what love means. He fears to love and loves to hate, and so he thinks that love is fearful, hate is love.
A Course in Miracles, Chapter 29, The Closing of the Gap

The timothy stands tall and cocky in the breeze, the fisted purple clover swollen and sharp as thistle. A wounded magpie trips along ahead—bitter and muttering—before, with one last gulp of courage, dodging into the brush. But there are predators in the grass, too, predators everywhere you look this off-kilter Colorado summer. In a normally drought-plagued month of rising fire danger weeds instead quadruple in size before my eyes, exploding with pollen. The ozone thins and rains batter, straining to cleanse the earth's toxins, poisons that run too deep to ever expunge.

"I am so over this," my daughter said, last night, in the hotel room, before slamming the door to go sleep with her friends.

We had just driven her and two of her teammates into Steamboat Springs for a three-day soccer tournament in which her U-16 team was participating. The two teammates (whose parents could not make it) had rented their own room. My daughter wanted to bunk with them, of course, but my husband and I had told her no. We had recently grounded her for lying about her whereabouts and our trust in her had plummeted. But when we arrived in Steamboat, my husband must have had a change of heart because he told her she could stay with the other girls before heading back downstairs to park the car in the garage across the street.

"Three teenage girls alone in a hotel room," the ego in my head shrieked. "What are you, crazy?"

There is really no upside to losing it with a teenager. The heated conversation that followed culminated in that great one-liner of hers that still reverberated in my head this morning as I walked the hills at the base of the ski mountain, searching for my right mind.

"I am so over this."

And I wondered how that could be? I had hiked these hills before, years earlier in another season, my daughter a light weight on my back, snow sucking at my ankles, back when I was her ankles. Her weight all at once doubling as the cradle of the backpack rocked her at last to sleep. Teething, she had not slept in days it seemed and neither had I. I might have walked to Wyoming if the cold had not made a run at my toes to the rhythm of the unconscious thud of her between the blades of my aching shoulders. In the condo we warmed our hands by the fire. I boiled noodles and frozen peas and mashed a banana. I dropped Cheerios like coins into the larger Cheerio of her mouth and we were happy again.

I am still carrying her but the weight has grown almost intolerable and the time has come to put her down. The aspen leaves tremble like a lip at the thought. I walk in that limbo I sometimes experience practicing forgiveness: the gap between recognizing the problem is not out there and allowing the solution; returned to the decision maker's driver seat again but not yet able to shift from neutral to drive.

I recall my behavior the night before, the way my anger at my husband and daughter morphed to include her friends, teammates, other parents, Republicans appearing to sabotage health care reform, a colleague who appeared to have betrayed me. I swear out loud at an ambush of mosquitoes and try to choose again, noticing once more that when I am not in my right mind I am wholly insane, absolutely convinced the world and everyone in it has turned on me. How it all comes down to a matter of trust. Not trusting my daughter because I can't trust the false self the ego created, the self I think I am, the self I think betrayed its parent's trust by forging off on its own. But this is not a self-help Course. There is nothing helpful about enabling the hero of a dream that despite the plot details *always* ends the same way.

How difficult this trust issue becomes when I listen to the ego, reigniting my own guilt about the choices I made as a young person, confusing those choices with the real choice that haunts my dream, the original choice to throw love away, the denied and mistaken belief I have murdered oneness and can never find it again. That void nips at my heels all the time in the world the ego made, the black hole into which I believe I fell from grace, enveloped by eternal nothingness rather than the eternal fullness of truth. I ask for help in looking at this but no one answers. Holy Spirit has gone missing again, I think, even though a part of me knows this cannot be.

> There is no time, no place, no state where God is absent…The
> compromise the least and littlest gap would represent in His
> eternal Love is quite impossible. For it would mean His Love
> could harbor just a hint of hate, His gentleness turn
> sometimes to attack, and His eternal patience sometimes fail.
> All this do you believe when you perceive a gap between your
> brother and yourself. How could you trust Him then? For He
> must be deceptive in His Love.

I assume my daughter is as untrustworthy as the self I think I
am; a self I believe cast away the gift of the one love we really are.
When I side with the ego, my love for my daughter is quite
impossible. When she defies my wishes, my false gentleness
turns to attack; my patience fails. I am deceptive in what I call
love in this dream and the ego rejoices because as long as I think
she has betrayed me, the one love we are has no chance in hell of
resurfacing in my mind. But when I step back, when I put the
burden of my special love down, when I ask the Holy Spirit to
help me remove the conditions I have written into the script to
keep the one love we are and have never really left away, my
mind heals. In that moment of healing, I again allow the
reflection of love that remains in my mind to shine.

By the time I return from my walk to meet my daughter and
her friends for breakfast before the first game, the Holy Spirit has
returned. I joke with the teenagers as we drive to the field,
marveling at the lush hills, the great inverted blue bowl of a sky,
a hawk circling with great purpose, the girls' witty repartee, my
husband's generosity. I am filled with gratitude that nothing dire
has occurred because I seemed to have once more turned away
from love. And yet somehow managed to find my way home
again once I allowed myself to accept what had really gone
AWOL.

The End of Specialness

Without foundation nothing is secure. Would God have left His Son in such a state, where safety has no meaning? No, His Son is safe, resting on Him. It is your specialness that is attacked by everything that walks and breathes, or creeps or crawls, or even lives at all. Nothing is safe from its attack, and it is safe from nothing.

A Course in Miracles, Chapter 24, The Forgiveness of Specialness

Awakening that first morning in the deep freeze of a dark, air-conditioned bedroom, it took me a moment to pick up the thread of the waking dream of separate interests *A Course in Miracles* teaches me I am living when I choose to listen to the ego. (That would be most of the time, or, at least, whenever I am not actively choosing to listen to the Holy Spirit/the part of my mind that remembers the one love I really never left.) But this first full day of vacation in a remote beach town nestled deep within the Yucatan, I believed I needed a break from forgiving. I neglected to ask what part of my mind had decided this as I brushed my teeth in the un-air-conditioned bathroom, immediately enveloped in a cloud of damp heat. We had arrived after dark the night before. There was a beach to explore right down those stairs and out that door, and I was burning daylight.

I paused a moment taking in the stillness of the swimming pool outside the sliding doors on the first floor of this lovely house. My husband and I had rented it through the internet from a charming American couple with whom we'd been chatting away about the wonders of the area for the last couple months. This fishing village was the real thing, we'd been told, not the Mexico of the sanitized compounds lining the Riviera we had long turned our noses up at. We have traveled before off the beaten track in this country, although our farthest flung adventures had been in the company of Mexican friends. We were flying solo here; relying on our daughter's scanty Spanish and my occasional enthusiastic if incomprehensible outbursts, our landlords' helpful emails, and a tiny, friendly expat community. We had come to partake with our daughter and her friend of the area's eco, historical, and cultural treasures while working in some serious beach time—a lot to cram into a week but that's just the kind of indefatigable, adventurous travelers we prided ourselves on being. I admired the way the pool water seamlessly met the aquamarine glow of the gulf in the distance before descending several stairs, opening the locked door, and stepping out onto the picturesque beach.

A boat painted the turquoise of retro kitchen appliances rocked gently on its anchor. In a puddle of pink light, two fishermen pushed out to sea. I slipped off my flip flops and began following the ragged shoreline, stepping over the lines of moored fishing boats, but soon disturbed by broken shells and worse, chards of glass, I put my shoes back on and retreated a little further inland. That's when my eyes, adjusting to the sensory overload that is Mexico, took in the trash mingled with seaweed washed up on shore: bottles and cans, plastic bags, and picnic refuse—a profusion of waste marring the white sand and sea grass—blown flush against the walls of an eclectic array of beach homes.

"Is this really what you had in mind?" the ego asked.

It had a point. I *had* wanted real Mexico, only, you know, complete with trash collection. It had been a long year recovering from a broken hip, the unstable economy, a greater than normal workload, immersion in several new promising but initially exhausting endeavors, my husband moving his business in a risky environment, fielding our teenage daughter's expertly pitched curveballs. But I had not come all this way to listen to the ego. I just wanted to be mindless for a while, having forgotten that is exactly the ego's preferred state, and that no good has or ever will come of it. Eager to get on with my vacation, I pushed my judgments aside, once again deceived there was actually something "out there" to sweep away. I wanted to get away from the ugliness of the ego I had been observing for so long, forgetting that looking at that ugliness without judgment with our inner teacher is exactly the process through which I begin to glimpse the true light beyond.

As our week wore on, my little fantasy of the perfect vacation began to unravel as all little fantasies in the ego's world of projected guilt do. During our tour of the ruins with a delightful Mayan English-speaking guide my daughter and her friend succumbed to the heat in the un-air-conditioned museum, stumbling along behind us like dying adolescent swans. The promised lobsters allegedly in peak season never materialized. The rainy season had muddied the waters of the famed network of cenotes we hoped to cool off in near the ruins and other inland destinations. My husband had one of his little meltdowns and he and our daughter spent several trying hours ignoring each other before he succumbed the next morning to a rapidly moving virus that left me fearing he might have contracted Swine Flu: a thought that launched the ego on a frantic, ignorant internal rant about the probable horrors of Mexican hospitals. Although guarded over by Federales with drawn weapons while we changed a flat tire, we did not feel secure. We got hopelessly lost in a nearby Colonial city where the highly recommended restaurant we finally found was inexplicably closed, our weak Colorado constitutions unable to rally the energy necessary to tour the historic plaza. On the last day, I contracted what would prove a week-long bout of Montezuma's revenge—the ego's final retaliation for our vacation's failure to meet its expectations.

Nevertheless, our holiday, like the lives we had left behind, offered moments of pure wonder. We spent a magic morning with a Mexican guide in a tiny boat but 500 feet or so from hundreds of preening flamingoes. A couple of nights the girls knocked themselves out at a carnival with vintage rides reminiscent of my childhood, where local teenage boys running the Tilt-O-Whirl darted in and out of the equipment, spinning them around by hand extra fast as my husband and I contemplated what OSHA might have to say. We partook of the kindness of a group of expats who welcomed us into their community with open arms, and everywhere we went, marveled at how hard people worked for so little. How bravely they went about their days without basic infrastructure such as trash collection, or the water and waste treatment services we completely take for granted. And we spent long afternoons recuperating from our ambitious, largely ill-fated plans, sprawled on a clean expanse of sand in a small adjacent city/Mexican tourist destination, swimming in that aquamarine water, eating ceviche, and sucking down frozen Mexican slurpee-like drinks.

It was on that beach on one of our last days—perched on a seven-mile long sandbar made when a meteor took out the dinosaurs all those years ago in the dream—that I momentarily glimpsed the end of specialness. The ego had been presenting a little review of all that had not gone well.

"It's not that any one of those things in and of themselves would be all that bad," it said. "I mean, a palmetto bug the size of a kitten, that moth in your face the size of a bat, the way the girls completely shun you. It's just the accumulation of them one on top of the other, you know: the way he always does this on vacation, the way she always does that."

I actually put my hands to my ears, as if the voice were coming from somewhere outside, instead of inside my head (as if I had a head). I really couldn't stand it anymore. Help me, I pleaded, silently, walking the pinkish sand, picking my way around perfectly happy seeming Mexican families chatting and building castles with their children, waiting for my right mind to click in, ready at last to forgive.

Once more, suddenly drenched by the swelter, I ventured into the tepid water and walked out a long way against the strong westward current. Waist deep, I began to swim parallel to it until, exhausted, I gave up, and turned to face the seven-mile long pier built to accommodate incoming ships. For a long time I floated, watching vehicles seemingly driving nowhere. All the vacations I had ever taken flashing through my mind, the early road trips with my parents, excursions with friends in my twenties, the adventures my husband and daughter and I had embarked on; peak moments and horror stories.

As I watched those cars and trucks driving out into the middle of the ocean, my desire for what would happen next in this dream completely washed away. My mind grew perfectly still. I watched. I listened. The sound of voices speaking a language I could not understand receded. *This is the end of the dream* came a voice in my mind. I realized the story of a special self that could only bring me pain was nearing its end. Nothing my husband, daughter, the weather, the exterminators, the government, my parents, my friends and neighbors, the Mexican tourists swimming around me could do could affect me in any way. I was suddenly catapulted beyond all desire. I truly wanted nothing. I totally understood that no one or thing outside my mind could bring me joy or pain. A comfort unlike any I have ever known, an overwhelming sense of grace shuddered through me. Tears stood in my eyes. For a moment, I had no idea who or what I was. And I was unalterably happy.

I must have been afraid, of course, because the moment passed. But it left me with a strengthened commitment to this path that teaches us to allow the undoing of our denied guilt over our addiction to what the Course calls our specialness, the unique, bogus individuality we covet over the expansive, unified love we are. On a remote bar of sand staring at a road that leads nowhere, once more observing the ego's agenda with my inner teacher, I experienced our innocence. And I vowed never to go on vacation with the ego without inviting my inner teacher again.

Heaven Is the Decision I Must Make

I've come to think of this as the summer of my discontent. Nothing has really worked. My life on every level appears to have taken a turn for the worse. Every day, sometimes every hour, with our teenage daughter seems to present another problem or demand another ambiguous decision. Our discussions about how to handle each challenge often erupt in confusion and disagreement. We are often overwhelmed and sometimes paralyzed by the fear of making a wrong decision.

An organization in which I am involved as a volunteer has presented non-stop drama. Efforts to mediate merely escalate flurries of attacking emails, verbal assaults, and unproductive meetings. Dependent on my daughter's work schedule and hours that never materialized, we postponed weekend camping trips and put other favorite summer activities on hold. Torrential rains prohibited more routine forms of summer recreation.

I am still physically recovering from an illness contracted during a vacation that for a number of reasons did not ultimately feel like one. We have indefinitely postponed the possibility of enabling our daughter to get a car pending currently absent signs of maturity. Although relieved that the school year is about to begin to provide us all with welcome structure, I am not looking forward to resuming my part-time job as chauffer to multiple, far-flung, required activities. In short, not only have I lost my sense of humor, I have started to believe in the nightmare of this world again. I have again forgotten I can choose from moment to moment—regardless of the plot details the script appears to throw at me—another teacher, provided I can remember I always have a choice to make, and that when I make it peace of mind returns, regardless of those plot details.

As workbook lesson 138 tells us, "Heaven is the decision I must make." *Heaven* being one of the Course's symbols for the one, eternal love we never left.

You need to be reminded that you think a thousand choices are confronting you, when there is really only one to make. And even this but seems to be a choice. Do not confuse yourself with all the doubts that myriad decisions would induce. You make but one. And when that one is made, you will perceive it was no choice at all. For truth is true, and nothing else is true. There is no opposite to choose instead.

Even though too often this summer it has not felt like I have a choice; even though sometimes I can't seem to remember my natural state in the dream *is* the ego thought system, a thought system that squelches the memory of the part of my mind that chose it in the first place. Why? Because it's very (seeming) existence relies on keeping me mindless. And the part of my mind that chose for the ego—terrified of annihilation—still favors this poor, pitiful individuality over deciding for the truth of what I am.

These mad beliefs can gain unconscious hold of great intensity, and grip the mind with terror and anxiety so strong that it will not relinquish its ideas about its own protection. It must be saved from salvation, threatened to be safe, and magically armored against truth.

Last week I was interviewed about forgiveness and special relationships for an upcoming movie about *A Course in Miracles*. Anyone who knows me also knows how trying my ego identity finds public speaking of any kind. In my desire to deepen my learning and accelerate the healing of my mind, I have begun teaching the Course, but that doesn't mean I have overcome my fear. Sitting in front of the camera, my body experienced all the usual unpleasant sensations—heart racing, sweaty palms, dry mouth, etc. And yet, as I began to answer each question, I lost consciousness of the body. Susan bowed out of the picture, allowing our one right mind to respond, utilizing the body for its only truly helpful purpose, that of a communication vehicle for the right rather than the wrong mind. In between questions, slipping back into the ego mind, the body's discomfort returned until I began answering the next question. The experience illuminated the dueling teachers the separated self believes it is choosing between; the way in which we are wholly sane or insane depending on which thought system we decide to allow. But it happened so rapidly I had no awareness that I had made a conscious choice, even though my alternating state of mind testified otherwise.

A Course in Miracles' forgiveness process invites us to recognize that what seems to be going on inside or outside the body we believe we inhabit has nothing to do with our true identity in the singular wholeness of Heaven, the unity we believe we destroyed in our hallucinated experiment in running away from home. Although I have made healing my mind through applying the Course's teaching my primary goal, I still often underestimate my unconscious investment in the ego's plan to "save" me from our Creator's retribution for a false crime I nevertheless believe I committed: a plan that involves engaging in a dualistic world of constant conflict that—although it will never bring me lasting joy or peace and will end in pain and death—promises to reinforce an autonomous identity complete with special characteristics, talents, and problems. While functioning as a figure in the dream, I continue to underestimate my fear of losing that identity and disappearing into a non-dualistic state, and I continue to forget I have a choice. That does not make me a bad *A Course in Miracles* student and teacher despite the ego's ravings. But it does make me a frightened one. I need to expose that fear and allow its undoing by choosing to look at it with my inner teacher.

In this insanely complicated world, Heaven appears to take

the form of choice, rather than merely being what it is. Of all the choices you have tried to make this is the simplest, most definitive and prototype of all the rest, the one which settles all decisions...But when you solve this one, the others are resolved with it, for all decisions but conceal this one by taking different forms.

There is only one problem: our belief in the idea of separation. And only one solution: withdrawing our belief by choosing again for our right mind. My dream has been quite dramatic lately, rapidly devolving before my body's eyes when I look with the ego. The more I ask for help from the Holy Spirit, the more challenges the ego seems to throw my way. But the ego is not my friend. It believes its own horrific story and has a huge investment in keeping me asleep. Yet the remedy for the ego's insanity remains in my mind, too, if I will only step out of the movie and remember I am the projector. If I will only take a single moment to remember I am the decision maker that can choose again for the antidote to the delusion of persecution by all those other actors who appear to keep me from realizing the love I am. If I will only ask my inner teacher for help in remembering that all my seeming attempts to fix things in the illusion will never work. It's like trying to explode bombarding asteroids hurtling toward me from all directions in one of those old video games. As soon as I destroy one; another is already taking me out in my peripheral vision until I forget I am only playing a game, and become completely invested in saving myself and the earth from certain destruction.

It will never work. If I insist on holding my daughter and husband, the personalities in the dysfunctional organization (oxymoron?), the economy, the weather, the parasite invading my body, my fear of embarrassment and failure responsible for my happiness, I am—like all other expressions of the ego in this dream of exile—doomed. But if I can look at all these special relationships with the Holy Spirit that remembers the truth in me, if I can choose again for our innocence and forgive myself when I am too afraid to do so, the summer of my discontent transforms into the greatest undoing of the thought system so far, and I come a little closer to gladly answering my call for love in you.

An Interview with the Holy Spirit

I've been giving the ego a lot of press lately in these pages. That's why I (the decision maker, the part of my mind that seemingly chose individuality over eternal wholeness and now seems to choose between the ego and the Holy Spirit) decided to interview the Holy Spirit (a lofty name for our memory of eternal wholeness) to get its take on a few important Course topics.

Me: Nice to have you on board; this is long overdue. The ego gets so much more attention around here—squeaky wheel and all that. Anyway, as you know *A Course in Miracles* tells us the one Son of God at some point had a "tiny mad idea." *What would it feel like to be on my own?* The very thought seemingly catapulted it outside wholeness. At that point the one mind seemed to split into the ego and the Holy Spirit, and the one son chose to believe the ego's lie that it had pulled off a kind of celestial homicide. Terrified of retribution and still curious to experience autonomy, the one mind appeared to fuse with the ego, metaphorically fell asleep, and followed it into a dream of duality. But even though we believe we inhabit these separate bodies complete with unique personalities in an illusory world of seemingly infinite differentiation, we have, in fact, never left the eternal, unified, oneness of our creator. Tell us, Holy Spirit, how could such a thing have happened?

Holy Spirit: What tiny mad idea?

Me: OK, well, let me restate this. According to the ego, it's not so much a tiny mad idea as a catastrophic event.

Holy Spirit: ☺

Me: I know, but according to the ego we pulled it off! Not only did we find ourselves out on the proverbial sidewalk, we believed we destroyed the house on the way out. So God—and I'm merely relaying the ego's story here—got totally pissed off and somehow rose from the dead and was already tracking us, see? So, the ego said we had to get the hell out and then I, the decision maker, believed it. Why? You may ask. I was afraid God would get me and also because I was still curious, you know, about this whole idea of autonomy and then—POOF! Everything exploded—what our scientists refer to as the big bang. So, suddenly we had this whole universe of fragmented forms, selves and problems; worries, drama, politics, disease, insects, war and me against you. It's exhausting to even talk about. Excuse me while I get some water.

Holy Spirit: ☺

Me: So I guess my question is the question almost every Course student asks sooner or later and usually right off the bat and that is: How could this have happened?

Holy Spirit: It didn't.

Me: Thank you. That's what I say, too, of course, except when my mind is, you know, on ego (like in that old anti-drug TV commercial where they show your brain on drugs frying in a pan like an egg), which is most of the time although at least since I've been doing the Course I have more and more moments when I actually remember I have a mind and turn to you and then I get my answer. Like right now when I ask you why this all seems so real here, this body and this life and this kid of mine and this husband and this dysfunctional organization and this bonehead that just about killed me on the freeway and you say:

Holy Spirit: ☺

Me: OK, so another thing that gets very mixed up for us Course students. Is it OK for me to ask you for help in this world?

Holy Spirit: What world?

Me: Right, but I mean, when I'm down and out, so to speak,

like in that Simon & Garfunkel song, *Bridge over Troubled Water*? Which I have to say always reminds me of you. Like when I need your help to solve this problem with my kid or my parent or loved one or boss, is it OK for me to just ask for a little favor now and then? Maybe just a little honest to God miracle in form.

Holy Spirit: ☺

Me: Alright, then I get what you're saying but it's just that sometimes, you know, Susan gets upset and—

Holy Spirit: Sometimes?

Me: Right, well, often Susan gets upset and—

Holy Spirit: Susan?

Me: See, you do have a sense of humor. So, the person I think I am that doesn't really exist in truth gets upset and can't remember what she is and it would just really help if you would say something like: "Susan, you've forgotten what you are again. Here's what you need to do to heal your relationship with _____."

Holy Spirit: What relationship?

Me: You're good, I've never doubted that.

Holy Spirit: ☺

Me: OK, well, that might be a slight exaggeration. Anyway, you're saying, and correct me if I'm wrong, you don't even know about me as an individual, and you're reminding me I don't really have any relationships in truth at the level of form. You're trying to tell me there is really only one relationship: my relationship with the one love I never left. And I remember that relationship and experience true peace when I join my mind with yours, which is really just the memory of our eternal wholeness that followed me into the dream?

Holy Spirit: Gigantic ☺

Me: Thank you. Thank you very much. So it sounds like what you're trying to tell me is you're not like some kind of fairy Godmother I can call on that descends into my dream sprinkling miracle dust or bonking this person that seems to be out there driving me crazy over the head with a magic wand. You're merely the other part of my seemingly split mind, the memory of what I truly am that followed me into the dream? And I can always experience peace of mind when I choose against the ego's lie that my happiness depends on what someone seemingly "out there" does or doesn't do to or for me?

Holy Spirit: ☺

Me: And I suppose you're also trying to tell me that I need to look at the world the ego made—itself a projection of the denied thought of guilt in the one son's mind, a result of its belief in having pulled off the separation—with you. Because that is the *only* way I will experience peace. If I try to look at the way I project my repressed guilt onto others, as the Course is teaching us we do whenever we judge, or the way I defend myself to avoid responsibility for the buried guilt in my mind without your help, I cannot experience the release forgiveness brings. I only end up feeling guiltier and blaming myself, which just strengthens my belief in the ego. But if I ask you for help in looking at all my interactions with others, allow you to gently remind me that I'm only dreaming and there is only one mind in need of healing, and turn my projection over to you, I experience deep comfort. In the holy instant of joining my mind with the part of my mind that is yours I fuse with our innocence.

Holy Spirit: ☺

Me: And the more I practice this process—the Course's definition of forgiveness—the more time I spend right-minded with you, until eventually I no longer listen to the ego and all my projections are undone. When all these blocks are gone, all that will remain is the one love I am and I awaken from the dream of this body/personality and its separate interests and am reunited forever with our wholeness.

Holy Spirit: ☺

Me: Well, I guess that's a wrap for today. I do love these conversations. They make me feel so special, you know?

Holy Spirit: Gigantic ☺

Choose To Demonstrate a Changed Mind About the World

Today I am thinking about the passing of Senator Edward Kennedy and what *A Course in Miracles* means by the term "teacher of God," someone who demonstrates the eternal, united love we mistakenly think we exchanged for these flimsy autonomous identities we cling to.

So let's start with flimsy, autonomous identities. I come from a long line of working class Irish Catholics who revered the Kennedys as Celtic, famine- and religious persecution-surviving superheroes. Dad and Mom worked on Jack Kennedy's presidential campaign and were even invited to the inauguration. They later made phone calls and rang doorbells for Bobby's (we called them all by first name in my house) senatorial and presidential race. They devoted a corner of our semi-finished basement to photographs of the clan (who I came to consider a reclaimed regal branch of the family tree) mixed in with a few choice grin and grips with the venerated duo. I still remember every detail of the morning I learned they shot Bobby, the monstrosity of a pink eyelet sundress I later wore to wait in line with my father and our parish priest for eight hours on a sweltering June day for the viewing at Saint Patrick's Cathedral; vendors hawking Bobby key chains and shot glasses; men and women of all ages and sizes and colors hiding their tears behind sunglasses. I didn't even try to hide mine listening to Teddy on TV at yet another funeral:

> My brother need not be idealized, or enlarged in death beyond what he was in life; to be remembered simply as a good and decent man, who saw wrong and tried to right it, saw suffering and tried to heal it, saw war and tried to stop it.

In 1980, in my early twenties and freshly transplanted to California, I worked as a volunteer for Ted's presidential bid despite my cynicism and disdain over rumors about his personal life as well as the horrific Chappaquiddick accident. Although he failed to land the nomination he went on to distinguish himself as perhaps the most cherished member of the U.S. Senate in recent memory, a passionate and unrelenting champion of the underdog, the oppressed, the suffering, the disabled and needy. Loved and respected by colleagues on both sides of the aisle, he worked for justice, surmounting personal tragedies and deep character flaws to demonstrate (the Course's synonym for teaching) true compassion. More often I think he modeled what the Course calls right-mindedness while negotiating for the common good, building bridges with opponents while never losing sight of ideals that—whether you agreed with his politics or not—were intended to benefit all.

"Seek not to change the world, but choose to change your mind about the world," *A Course in Miracles* tells us. But too often we Course students misinterpret this quote, a result of what the Course calls "level confusion." Many Course students brag about how they do not vote or purchase insurance, how they refrain from watching the TV news or participating in organizations. Some ignore their health, stop seeing doctors, quit their jobs and stop paying bills. If the world and the bodies in it are illusions, they reason, why bother? But is there really anything spiritual about turning your back on normal human responsibilities? And if you withdraw from interacting, where does that leave what the Course calls our classroom? Where does that leave the curriculum comprised of our relationships with other people and situations that appear to compromise our peace the Course teaches us to use to undo our belief in the world and the content of guilt it seeks to mask?

Certainly, at the non-dualistic level of truth, we have never left the one love we are, and need not concern ourselves with an illusory world created to make the errant belief of separation real. On the level of form at which we operate, however, seemingly marooned in separate bodies with separate interests, we must deal with the world. We do it every time we draw a breath, eat, sleep, touch, drive, listen, speak, blink, work, attack, defend, acknowledge or ignore a loved one or enemy.

On the level of form in which we believe we operate (and most of the time even Course students believe this or we wouldn't be here), what we do or do not do in this world depends on which inner teacher we (the decision maker) have chosen as our guide: the ego or the Holy Spirit/right mind. When we choose the ego its thought system of separation and exclusion determines our actions and reactions. We experience an unstable, threatening, often incomprehensible world filled with competing interests. But when we actively choose to listen to the Holy Spirit, we experience a stable state of mind invulnerable to the ego's scare tactics. We experience only common interests, and seek common interests in all our interactions. Our right mind informs our actions without a sense of straining to solve problems and we do not exclude anyone at the level of our mind, even as we go about relating in a differentiated environment. We have remembered with our inner teacher that there is always only one problem: the belief in separation; and always only one solution: bringing the darkness of our guilty projections/illusions to the innocent light of our right mind.

Our roles and vocations in the world do not really matter. We can demonstrate right-mindedness as a factory worker, as a nurse, as an artist, as a parent, as a prisoner, as an illegal alien or as a United States Senator. But it takes work because we are terrified by the denied guilt in our mind. As it surfaces again and again and our discomfort increases, our impulse to get rid of it (projection) seems irresistible because the ego's very existence depends on keeping our problem "out there." That's why it fights so hard to perpetuate its attack/defense cycle that prevents us from accessing the part of our one mind that can choose again. But it is only a belief. And while we navigate this world of form, we can learn to receive the Course's gift of forgiveness, to use the process that enables us to undo our belief in the ego's lie from moment to moment until our mind permanently heals and we awaken forever to whole, eternal love.

I can't pretend to know what was going on in Ted Kennedy's mind over these last few decades as he worked for social justice. But I do believe he often demonstrated the Course's practice of forgiveness, rising again and again above the battleground by choosing the right mind, even as he *engaged* in an inherently divisive and increasingly polarized political arena. Whatever the form of his spirituality; the universal content of allowing the Holy Spirit to remove our belief in separate interests remains the same. And because there is only one mind in need of healing, we are all a little closer to awakening for his willingness.

His final words to Bobby seem a fitting tribute to him as well:

Those of us who loved him and who take him to his rest today, pray that what he was to us and what he wished for others will someday come to pass for all the world.

May this world of separate interests continue to pass away as we accept our common ground.

Above All Else I Want the Peace of God

Before those of you unfamiliar with the Course (who are, like me, organized religion-challenged), get too worked up over the G word, let me explain that we should read this work—as premier scholar Ken Wapnick advises—as we would a great epic poem. Teeming with metaphor, *A Course in Miracles* reinterprets familiar Christian terminology just as it reinterprets everything else we think we understand in this world. The word "God," for example, symbolizes the non-dualistic, eternal love we truly are, a love that transcends our current understanding. It refers to that state prior to the birth of the ego thought system that created this illusory, dualistic universe filled with individual identities and competing interests. The word "God" in the Course has nothing to do with the God most of us were brought up with, an unstable entity created by the ego in its own unstable image.

OK, now that I got that out of the way, let me repeat:

Above all else I want the peace of God.

I am coming to a place in my practice of the Course's unique form of forgiveness where I recognize I will never find happiness in this world for very long, and that even fleeting happiness comes with conditions too painful to meet. I have just completed another novel, for example, and am currently querying multiple agents to try to convince them to read my manuscript and hopefully offer representation. If and when that happens, they will begin the arduous task of querying publishers to find someone willing to bring my manuscript into the world.

Although excited about my new book, I am also realistic about the daunting odds. When I started writing fiction in my early thirties, I was considered a young novelist; today, well, not so much. I have had three very capable agents representing three other "promising" manuscripts that for one reason or another, never yielded book contracts (and these in a relatively thriving economy).

In the past, my elated only to be deflated ego rode the roller coaster of these experiences in its usual state of terrified exhilaration, convinced it had transferred its identity to 350 or so double-spaced, laser printed, 9 ½ x 11 pages of text, its flaming littleness exposed. This time around, I can no longer accept this fate, not because anything external has changed but because I am at a point in my journey where I want out of this dream of exile more than I want in. Increasingly more. I am realizing as I begin to relive the serendipitous nature of seeking a publisher that no matter what the outcome it cannot bring me what I truly long for, can never appease that ancient longing only the G word's peace can.

Above all else I want the peace of God.

Workbook lesson 185, "I want the peace of God,", begins:

> To say these words is nothing. But to mean these words is everything... No one can mean these words and not be healed. He cannot play with dreams, nor think he is himself a dream. He cannot make a hell and think it real. He wants the peace of God, and it is given him. For that is all he wants, and that is all he will receive...

I have added the words "Above all else" to the beginning of this lesson in hopes that stating my intention, making this my *primary* goal, will help me focus my ever-wavering attention on just how much the part of me that chooses would still love to see the ego's plan for salvation work. If I could have my specialness, my Susan-ness, and still revel in earthly bliss; if my intimate relationships could just memorize their lines in their Harlequin romance and Hallmark movie scripts; if my writing career could finally realize its intended meteoric trajectory and deliver the goods I deserve after all the hours I've clocked; if this body could just cooperate with my fountain-of-youth fantasies; if I could just have my Course and find enduring success and happiness here in this world, too.

Just because I am at a place where I want out of the dream more than I want in, just because I am currently in a state of diminished fear about the consequences of truly relinquishing thoughts of judgment, victimization, and uniqueness and disappearing into the one love we are, does not mean I have given up my attraction to the ego's game of seek but do not find. But it does mean the part of my mind that chooses between the ego and the Holy Spirit, liberated through the day-in-and-day-out practice of forgiving its belief about all it experiences and thereby no longer seemingly fused with the ego, is always watching. It does mean the chooser in my mind is growing stronger each time it experiences the peace available when it chooses to allow the right mind to *undo* its defenses against love. It does mean the chooser is beginning to associate its choice for the ego with pain and its choice for the Holy Spirit (the memory of the one love we are that calls us to awaken) with peace. And to recognize that the Course means what it says when it tells us the two seeming voices cannot speak over one another. When we listen to the ego, we are completely screwed, no matter how petty the specific problem or how promising the specific solution. When we listen to the Holy Spirit, there is no problem no matter how monumental the world would measure our challenge.

I have added the phrase "Above all else" to the beginning of this lesson because I am beginning to realize that although the Course tells us we need only a little willingness to forgive, I believe that is only an introductory phase. It takes only a little willingness to begin reading *A Course in Miracles* and suspend our disbelief about its fantastic claims as we do when we enter a great work of fiction. But it takes increasing willingness, vast willingness (what the Course calls vigilance) to truly walk its talk.

Applying the Course's principles goes far beyond reciting its beautiful affirmations. It means setting a priority for what we really want and long for beyond the ego's shabby promises. It means putting the peace of God always at the forefront of our attention while observing with our inner teacher just how much we still cling to our specialness and forgiving that, too. It means learning to ask our inner teacher in every lesson that arises in the seeming classroom of our lives what we really want beyond the ego's addictive, self-defeating interests. When I do this, I realize that although the circumstances of my life have relative importance, they will never bring me what I want. This understanding will free me forever from the bondage of the ego thought system, if I let it. From here, as the Course tells us again and again, we cannot fail, as long as we remember to take the proverbial hand of our proverbial guide.

Above all else I want the peace of God.

My growing willingness accelerates my return to truth as I turn to my inner guide for help in changing my mind about the bogus possibility of arriving at the peace the G word promises without releasing the agents, editors, clients, children, parents, and spouses the ego would have me believe both support and thwart me. Again and again and as long as needed, I remember what I really want and rediscover what I really am by changing my mind about you.

Let Me Recognize My Problems Have Been Solved

Don't take life too seriously. You'll never get out alive!
Bugs Bunny

The persona I keep forgetting I am not is such a drama queen. My father used to call her Sarah Bernhardt after the silent film melodrama star. My junior high friends called her Crusader Rabbit after the vintage cartoon character and sometimes, Susan of Arc for her impassioned pleas on behalf of truth, justice, and the American way. Fortunately, I have no idea what choice terms her enemies came up with.

The thing is; I have always taken everything so freaking personally. We all do, of course; it is the ego's way, but throughout my time on this planet I have perfected the art of suffering on behalf of myself and others to the level of fine art. (How "special" is that? ☺) I am a shining star in a galaxy of glowing orbs that have laid their hearts on the line for love and goodness, temporarily believing their darkness effectively eclipsed. But I am so tired of the whole celestial charade.

Let me recognize my problems have been solved.

The persona I keep forgetting I am not awoke this morning

overcome with the problem of its secret, enduring unworthiness, unloved and unloving, fluttering its empty sleeves as in a Wallace Stevens poem I have long admired. But the decision maker in my mind that almost always now watches these bodily theatrics did not choose to indulge it. It remembered it wanted the peace of God, a goal it has identified only after years of mindlessly choosing its opposite, and, with the Course's help, finally learning it had another choice and a mind outside the dream capable of choosing. And so it cried out for help. And the Holy Spirit answered. "Let me recognize my problems have been solved," it (metaphorically) said, quoting workbook lesson 80. Reminding me again that there is always only one problem: our belief that we have separated from our source. And always only one solution: recognizing the preposterous nature of this belief with our inner teacher.

Later, after seeing my daughter and husband off, I sat down at my desk and took a moment to once more connect with that light in my real mind and ask again for guidance. Then I randomly opened *A Course in Miracles* as I often do and read these words:

"Let me recognize my problems have been solved." I am not making this up; there it was again—one problem, one solution. The separation from the one love we are, the ego would have us believe we pulled off, never happened! In the instant the thought of running away from home arose in the one mind, it was immediately corrected. You cannot fragment whole love, this seemingly endless dream in which we find ourselves notwith-standing. None of it is real and the problem is already solved. We can continue to wage our ultimately defeating cartoon battles or we can open our eyes. And so, I decided to suspend my disbelief long enough to embrace this possibility. Because while the pull of the tear-jerker movie of Susan is strong, let's face it; I know only too well how it ends. Besides, the decision maker's growing commitment to realize the peace of God in an eternal identity beyond Susan is stronger.

"You are entitled to peace today," I read. "A problem that has been resolved cannot trouble you. Only be certain you do not forget that all problems are the same. Their many forms will not deceive you when you remember this."

Despite my problems' many guises, their nature never deviates. The underlying content of guilt over a separation that never happened remains the same. If I am feeling anything other than peace of mind, I have chosen to believe the ego's lie of competing interests in which someone always wins and someone always loses, just as it believes it triumphed at our creator's expense. Recognizing the one problem and allowing the one solution completely simplifies, orders, and brings meaning to an otherwise meaningless, chaotic existence.

"Yeah, right," the ego (metaphorically) said, emerging onto the screen of my perception seemingly out of left field, rolling its eyes like Bugs Bunny in the old aptly named *Looney Tunes*. A long, largely one-sided argument about the maddening characteristics of a particular individual currently making things exceptionally difficult for the persona I still, at times, believe I am and the personas I still at times believe my loves ones are ensued. But I am finally learning that arguing with the ego is no more productive or sane than conversing with animated rabbits. And I am learning that I cannot find the peace of God if I forgive everyone and everything else in my current dream except this particular individual, however tempted I am to make an exception based on his over-the-top, apparently unwarranted behavior.

The Course is not asking us to excuse or deny bad behavior. But it *is* asking us to recognize the reflection of the over-the-top, apparently unwarranted idea of separation when it arises in the classroom of our lives. It *is* asking us to recognize there is only one ego/wrong mind and only one Holy Spirit/right mind on the level of truth. My attempt to exclude this seemingly more difficult person or situation from the one love available, when I choose my right mind, prevents me from experiencing that love. I am merely reenacting the original decision to exclude God that got me into this illusory mess of a world to begin with. And it hurts.

Salvation lies *outside* the dream. So does the truth of what I am. So does the truth of this particular, irrational, at times even, frightening personality. I am finally learning that I cannot awaken if I draw a line in the sand between myself and anyone else. I must recognize the fear and hatred emanating from this seeming nemesis as my own, remember what I really want, and choose again. With the Holy Spirit's help, I learn to look past the content of his behavior in this illusion we seem to be navigating to the one love we share. If I deny its presence in him, I deny it in myself and continue to feel secretly unworthy, unloved and unloving, despite the crusading mask I present to the world. In that moment of recognition of the one self I am, I remember and receive the endless comfort of true love. I am relieved of the backbreaking burden of my personal resentment, undoing a little more unconscious guilt in the process. My grip on the ego thought system loosens. And I recognize, and at least for a while believe, that my problems have been solved.

Now I am able to take whatever steps may be needed on the level of form to address the behavior while simultaneously recognizing with our inner teacher that the ego's vicious attacks can, in truth, threaten nothing real. And that nothing the ego has seemed to pull off can ever truly alter the everlasting innocence we all share.

Another Blissful Conversation with the Ego

It's been a rough few days here in forgiveness land. Ever since I wrote about making the peace of God my primary goal, the ego has been relentless in its request for equal time from the decision maker (DM), the part of our mind that chooses between the ego's story of separation and the Holy Spirit's memory of unity. Of course the DM can always choose not to grant it. But, as I've mentioned before, attempts to censor the ego only seem to exacerbate its inevitable backlash. *A Course in Miracles* reminds us that you have to truly recognize the "enemy" and its ugly (albeit nonsensical) ways, before you can recognize you never really had one. So I am allowing the ego to speak with the DM, what's left of it, at least. After all, it has chosen not to access the Holy Spirit/right mind in days and is once more beginning to forget it has a mind. ☺

Ego: Above all else you want the peace of God? Seriously? Have we even met?

DM: OK, I'll admit I may have overstated things a tad.

Ego: You think?

DM: Alright, currently as it turns out, I do not want the peace of God above all else. I want fame, fortune, flourless chocolate cake, a glass of sauvignon blanc, and revenge, not necessarily in that order.

Ego: Damn straight! I saw the way you looked at your husband this morning. And you sat at that computer until midnight the other night drafting responses to those emails you were too chicken to send. That person deserves everything you wrote, by the way. No one in this universe can blame you for defending yourself from a complete maniac.

DM: Can I quote you on that?

Ego: Pock, pock, pock, pock.

DM: Right.

Ego: Better than happy, I always say.

DM: You are still quite quotable.

Ego: Well, that's one of the biggest understatements of all time.

DM: I seriously doubt that.

Ego: Really, Ms. "above all else I want the peace of God." So let me just ask you then why you've been in such a little hissy fit for the past five days?

DM: OK, you win. Currently, as it turns out, I definitely do not want the peace of God. I want to sit here engaging in this inane conversation because at least it allows me to keep this puny special identity intact.

Ego: Could you repeat that, I couldn't quite hear you.

DM: Currently, as it turns out—

Ego: No! The part before that—the *you win* part. Music to my ears—I could listen to that tune the rest of my life.

DM: God only knows.

Ego: Ha! OK, so, sorry to interrupt you on such a sweet roll. As you were saying, you currently do not want the peace God.

DM: Correct. Currently, as it turns out, I want pointless conversations with imaginary beings, judgment, exclusion, sarcasm, moral superiority, self-loathing, and self-righteousness. Sounds contradictory, I know, but that's the mind on ego for you.

Ego: Hey, when have I had anything but your best interests at heart?

DM: You don't really want me to answer that do you?

Ego: Hold on just one cotton picking minute, Susan.

DM: That's DM.

Ego: Yeah, *right*. Look, I've been doing my damndest to keep this from you but you're clearly getting pretty freaking smitten with this whole waking up delusion so I suppose you leave me no choice. Repeat after me. I DO NOT want the peace of God. GOD IS NOT MY FRIEND. God wants me seriously wacked. Why wouldn't he; I wacked him. Coming back to you now? It was a blood bath, I'm telling you.

DM: So you've mentioned a few billion times. God a la Tony Soprano. But the right mind has a different version.

Ego: Oh, let me guess: *It never happened.* Is he like a broken record or what? I mean, is that not the most childish, moronic argument in the universe? *Sticks and stones may break my bones but words.* That dude hasn't had an original thought in how many years?

DM: Hmmm. Original thought. Interesting choice of phrase.

Ego: What's that supposed to mean?

DM: Just that I hear lusting after originality is what started this whole mess of separate interests in the first place.

Ego: You're a mess of a separate interest.

DM: I'd like to believe that, if only it didn't make me feel so queasy.

Ego: I'll tell you what's making you feel queasy. The guilt over what you did, that's what. And what he wants to do back. But I'm telling you, if you'll just stick with me down here and forget about listening to that other crybaby that's just a figment of your tortured imagination for a minute you'll be fine. Trust me.

DM: Wow, déjà vu.

Ego: What?

DM: *Trust me.*

Ego: You got to trust someone, kid.

DM: Now *that's* good advice. Maybe it's time to once again start trusting that still small voice within.

Ego: Now why in hell would you do that?

DM: Because it makes me feel better; I remember now.

Ego: Don't do it, DM!! It'll strike you dead; I'm telling you! Don't go there, I'm warning you. You'll be sorry. I'm just trying to save your butt. I'm just trying...Can you hear me? DMmmmmmmmm!

DM: ☺

Above the Battleground

The town I grew up in has long staked its reputation on a revolutionary war battle waged by Mad Anthony Wayne: leader of a light infantry that stormed British fortifications camped out on the Hudson River under cover of darkness. The victory has long symbolized a psychological turning point for American forces, the beginning of the end of the war. Many townspeople so revere the general's courage and audacity that they reenact the hillside ambush each year in period garb before engaging in festivities designed to further commemorate our eventual autonomy from the tyranny of Mother England.

As a little girl, I would join the boys in the woods to reenact the famous battle; although we knew very little about it save that it involved people called red coats versus people called colonists. "Give me liberty or give me death," we shouted. (We drew straws for who got to play the red coats.) The boys let me impersonate a soldier because they were short on men; I wore my hair short, and despite my lack of heft, threw a mean punch. Later, when we reenacted World War II, however, they forced my girlfriend and me to play Japanese prisoners, a role I quickly tired of. And I soon enough discovered that no matter what historical conflict we attempted to emulate, we always ended up fighting each other, loyalties blurred, betrayals mounting, hurt feelings running rampant. Sooner or later, everyone started crying or screaming, someone got a bloody nose, someone else called in an adult, and we all found ourselves banished in shame to our private quarters. My mother would lower us into a hot bath, as if trying to scald away our baser natures.

I have been thinking about battles and battlegrounds lately— children's and adults'—and what *A Course in Miracles* means when it talks about "rising above the battleground." I have been thinking about battles and battlegrounds because I have been engaged on the perennial battleground like everyone else on this planet since my arrival, striving to prove my innocence relative to everyone else's greater guilt; attempting to triumph over everyone else's efforts to usurp my authority.

Applying *A Course in Miracles'* forgiveness to the seeming battles that arise in my everyday life—from apparently trivial traffic encounters to monumental-seeming issues in my closest relationships—has helped me begin to generalize the undoing of my belief in competing interests. I am beginning to see that the

Course means what it says when it tells us "there is no hierarchy of illusions" and "no order of difficulty in miracles." The former statement means that *everything* I experience outside my mind, without exception, is merely a projection of my belief that I have separated from my source/the one love I forever am. The latter statement means that the change of mind realized when I choose to shift from the ego's perception of competing interests to the Holy Spirit's message of perfect unity, corrects every seeming misperception that appears to disturb my peace. But I must learn to apply forgiveness to *all* my encounters, and, as the Above the Battleground section of Chapter 23 points out, some still seem more real than others: "...for your forgiveness of your brother is not complete as yet, and so it cannot be extended to all creation."

This is not a path in relativism. What's true is true, according to the Course; while what's false is false. Only knowledge/heaven/perfect, eternal love is true. *Everything* outside that truth is false. Since I am dreaming a dream of exile from truth, everything I experience within this body and without this body is false. Sounds simple except that we have no memory of our awakened state, unless we actively choose for our right mind/Holy Spirit: the part of our mind that holds the memory of waking wholeness for us in the dream.

As the teaching tells us again and again, we experience the undoing of the ego as a process in which we learn to apply forgiveness to *everything* that appears to arise to upset us, *everything* we believe interferes with our ability to preserve our ultimate autonomy and relative innocence. As we turn our frightening, dark illusions over to the light of our right mind, we experience deep relief/the return of endless comfort. By learning to watch the ego from the perspective of the decision maker in our mind with help from our loving inner teacher, we begin to realize how much pain the ego thought system's dynamic of attack and defense (designed to keep our guilt over the belief that we destroyed our creator alive by blaming it on someone else while avoiding responsibility for it) really costs us. And yet, as a new form of attack appears to arise, a vicious, unprovoked assault seems intent on destroying us, we may find ourselves once again clinging to our self-imposed bondage and plotting to break free. The belief in our invulnerability our right mind holds flies out the window as we turn once more to the body's eyes for clues to what's happening to us this time, and what we must do to protect ourselves/retaliate.

The belief that we pulled off the "crime" of separation runs deep in us. So does our intoxication with the original "tiny mad idea" of experiencing individuality. Our repressed fear of punishment is as great as our attraction to what the Course calls our "specialness." No wonder it sometimes seems that the more we forgive and experience the transformative peace of mind forgiveness brings, the more inventive the ego becomes in generating complicated, confusing, and traumatic dramas: fictions that enable us to act out our secret wish to be unfairly treated; a wish that keeps the battleground intact, the game in play, and the fabrication of individuality preserved.

And yet, the Course tells us, regardless of the size, scope, or seeming severity of the circumstances we perceive ourselves embroiled in, we can learn to rise above even the bloodiest battleground. I am reminding myself again of this idea because I need to hear it. I have felt victimized by a person and situation in my seeming world for a while now. I keep watching my ego's attachment to that idea, and asking for help in looking beyond the illusory form to the content beyond the dream. When I do, I realize I am simply witnessing the ego thought system we all share on a rampage. When I don't, specifically directed anger and fear raise their ugly heads, and I am once more catapulted into believing I am forgiving something real, rather than the antics of the split mind on ego. The ego's assaults, at times, have seemed so fast and furious I can barely catch my breath long enough to remember I have a mind that can choose to witness its projections without judgment; a mind that perceives the battle but recognizes it for the simple reenactment of the original battle it represents; a battle that never took place, rendering its reenactment ultimately impossible.

This is your part; to realize that murder in any form is not your will. The overlooking of the battleground is now your purpose.

The Course makes no distinction between minor irritation and murder because every loss of peace stems from the original thought of claiming our independence at our creator's expense. Whatever the problem on the level of form, the solution remains forgiveness, bringing the problem back to our mind and choosing again for the vision of our inner teacher that sees the illusion but does not take it seriously. But how do we overlook the battle-ground even as we take necessary steps on the level of form to address a potentially threatening situation? I have been asking this question these last few weeks, as I feel the constant pull to defend the little self I think I am and the little selves around me I love and befriend. *A Course in Miracles* tells us we can rise above the battleground by paying attention to the way we feel.

There is a stab of pain, a twinge of guilt, and above all, a loss of peace. This you know well. When they occur leave not your place on high, but quickly choose a miracle instead of murder.

I have gotten pretty good at choosing my right mind when confronted by a stab of pain or twinge of guilt but not so much when confronted by an apparent slanderous attack or unpro-voked act of cruelty. In this situation, because a part of my mind still upholds the childish notion of a hierarchy of illusions, I can't seem to catch myself in time. I am back on the battleground before I know what hit me. But when I take a moment and pause, as I have trained myself to do, I can retrace my steps back to my original decision to choose separation over eternal peace at the root of all subsequent reenactments from trivial to catastrophic. I can call on my awakened mind for its interpretation, allowing it to softly rain down on my mistaken awareness, washing away the hurt that battling illusions always brings.

I have chosen the Course's forgiveness to lead me home. I only need to keep practicing and choosing again to experience the miracle of changed perception. This situation has offered me an extraordinary lesson in healing my mind by demonstrating just how invested I am in preventing my own healing by believing in the circumstances of my unfair treatment. But as I have continued to ask my right mind to remember my true purpose, I find myself growing weary of my role in this reenactment. I feel much calmer today, almost ready to grow out of this, perhaps even ready to shed this period garb with our inner teacher's gentle smile and let the ego find another seeming actor to play out its wishes, peacefully aware that we all grow out of it in the end.

I Do Not Know the Self I Am

"Seek not to change the world" *A Course in Miracles* tells us in the opening of Chapter 21. "But choose to change your mind about the world." But changing my mind about the world takes lots of practice. My small world has been rocked in the past few months by the behavior of an individual who appears to embody all the ego thought system's darkness, that cesspool of sin, guilt, and fear the Course teaches us we spend our lives trying to disown. He lies, blames, cheats, bullies and threatens. He accuses me and others of complete fabrications. He has consistently demonstrated instability and mal intent and yet his false accusations continue to rankle. I have, at times, felt guilty over my inability to solve the problem, which seems to worsen by the minute. I have tried to remind myself that he is merely a projection of my own belief in guilt (as the Course teaches) and have called on our inner guide again and again but haven't really heard an answer that sustains me for very long. This person's actions and the crazy scenario they seem to have triggered appear all too real, relentless, and even frightening. And they have forced me to really examine what's going on with my compromised peace of mind.

When I say, as I did a couple weeks ago, "Above all else I want the peace of God," it is easy to forget that I am the peace of God. But that is the truth I am really defending so vigorously against. Because if I am the peace of God/the one love we have never really left, I am not the self I think I am, a self that can be worn down by, or strive to triumph over, difficult circumstances, events and individuals.

I do not know the self I am. This is the place I must return to again and again.

I cannot recognize my true identity beyond the ego's antics because I cannot find it in my own mind. I cannot find it in my own mind because I still think I, Susan, actually have a mind. I cannot find it in my own mind because I deliberately forgot it when I followed the ego into the dream of this world designed to uphold the impossible but tantalizing idea of autonomy from my source, and to keep me so distracted fielding incoming, imaginary attacks on a false identity that I forget I already have the peace I am. I cannot find it in my own mind because I believe the ego's lie that I have forever destroyed our creator, and can only prove my relative innocence by projecting that horrific guilt onto someone else.

I have been looking for myself in all the wrong places; the peace I am cannot simultaneously exist along with this false identity; an identity dependent on the whims of everyone and thing around it. That is the ego's secret understanding and terror, and why it so relentlessly clings to its story of persecution. But however convincing, its theatrics disappear when I choose to overlook our erroneous projection of guilt/anger/hatred without self-judgment but with the help of our inner teacher. The self I think I am cannot accomplish this alone. Without that help from the gentle, loving part of our mind that sees this world and its illusions but fails to take them seriously, we simply feel more guilty, project that guilt outside ourselves again, and experience its return in the form of someone else's attack.

I have spent the last several years actively practicing forgiveness *A Course in Miracles* style, consciously spending more and more time with the part of my mind that chooses between the ego and the Holy Spirit and watches the ego's dynamics. I still project, but when I do, instead of finding temporary solace, I experience almost instant pain. The defense/attack cycle designed to short-circuit our rebounding guilt by blaming others has collapsed. This particular saga has actually exposed a deeper layer of guilt in my mind that feels quite devastating, closer than ever to the original remorse and terror that arose in the one mind when it believed in its "tiny mad idea" of running away from home. "I am so sorry," a part of my tortured mind seems to chant because I can't fix the problem "out there" with my forgiveness, having once again fallen into the trap of believing I am forgiving something *real* in need of fixing, rather than a character in a morality play no more real, guilty, or innocent than the self I think I am.

Yesterday I called a good friend—a Course teacher I revere—to discuss this dilemma of guilt I seem to find myself mired in over this situation. Through the gift of silence, true listening, she helped me quiet my mind enough to embrace the answer. As a Course student and someone committed to awakening from this dream, it is not my job to save the world from the ego. But it is my job to withdraw my belief in the ego and a world in need of saving. I am not asked to rescue anyone or thing simply because—in truth—there is no one or thing in need of rescuing. The monsters in the closet, the ranting shadows on the wall simply reflect the fear of retribution we all share over a sin we never committed.

"I am so sorry," a part of my confused mind has chanted throughout this ordeal: an apology to my creator, really, for my belief that I destroyed him. But when I admit I do not know the self I am, when, motivated by my pain I turn this darkness over to the light in my right mind, it burns away. As I hold my projection harmless in this light, I am held harmless. My mind heals and all the urgent striving to solve the problem vanishes. I merely proceed with whatever necessary action reveals itself without malice toward anyone, including myself.

Or, I choose to do nothing, because the ego thought system expressed in this seeming individual's attacks will likely continue with or without my participation. Certainly, as the Course makes very clear, defending myself only fuels the ego's case. In the end whatever action I decide to take or not take on the level of form has no real value or meaning unless I first take right action in my mind. As always, that means forgiving: withdrawing my belief in the ego's power to threaten in any way the peace I am and recognizing with my right mind that we are one, regardless of seeming appearances. Only then does renewed compassion born of renewed awareness that we share the same guilty burden, the same tortured mind and the same path of redemption return. A guilty burden we can learn to put down, a tortured mind we can learn to heal, and a path of redemption we can learn—through the deep comfort it offers—we really do want to follow.

I Loose the World from All I Thought It Was

A few months ago I got hooked on the Dish network's Earth Channel broadcasting a twenty-four-hour feed of earth images taken by a camera mounted on the EchoStar 11 satellite and set to a soundtrack of 60's, 70's, and 80's tunes. Trippy classics like Jefferson Starship's *Miracles*, Yes' *Roundabout*, and Jethro Tull's *Aqualung* transported me back to a former life decades before I had any intention of forgiving anyone by traditional or radically alternative means; back to when I was merely an ego in a boom cycle thrashing its way through the minefield of attack and defense we call living, dodging imaginary incoming shrapnel and firing off a few highly justified and targeted grenades of my own.

My husband and daughter couldn't quite fathom my enthusiasm for the new cable channel, and even expressed mild concern over my growing obsession.

"So what does it *do*?" my husband asked.

"It's not so much about it doing anything," I said.

"OK." He backed away; disappeared into the vault of his office.

"The stoners at my school watch that channel all the time, *Mom*," my daughter said.

"And yet I grasp it without the aid of any mind-altering substances," I pointed out.

Her brows shot up the way they do. She assumed the maternal impersonation she sometimes adopts which can seriously creep me out if I let it, hugging herself and leaning back against the kitchen counter, patiently enduring yet another opportunity in which to suffer fools.

"Don't you have somewhere you're supposed to be?" I asked.

I soon learned that if you hit the pause button while cooking dinner and then hit play a half hour later you can train yourself to spot infinitesimal changes in the pattern of swirling gasses etched across our planet's face that usually resembles the profile of a woman emerging from the gnarl of an ancient tree. Her expression subtly morphs throughout the day and evening, exhausting the gamut of human emotions. This got me thinking about the purpose of this world and its exhausting emotions according to *A Course in Miracles*, which got me thinking about a meditation I read or heard somewhere, possibly Buddhist. You visualize your living space and those you live with and mentally state something like: "May everyone in this house be well and happy." Gradually moving outward, you go on to bless everyone in your neighborhood, your city, your country, the earth, the solar system and finally the universe. The idea seems to be to envelop all that exists in the wellness and happiness you visualize for yourself. It's a sweet meditation all too easily abandoned, I found, once I opened my eyes, uncrossed my legs and headed back out into the jungle.

I am thinking about the Dish Earth Channel's version of our planet viewed from outer space because it symbolizes the world to me, a world I can no longer view for long in the same way I used to thanks to *A Course in Miracles*. Despite its occasional, seductive entertainment value, whether viewed from a satellite or the seemingly flat ground I appear to traverse, my under-standing of the world's purpose and my own has begun to shift despite my formidable resistance to doing what our right mind asks us to do: withdraw our belief that an illusory world of form can in any way affect our state of mind.

A Course in Miracles workbook lesson 132, "I loose the world from all I thought it was," compares and contrasts our perception of the world based on which inner teacher's viewpoint we have chosen to believe, the ego or the Holy Spirit's. The Course tells us again and again that the world of perception we find ourselves navigating is an ego-generated illusion, a literal projection of the guilt in our one mind over our belief that we have pulled off the impossible by dividing the eternally whole and indivisible. The ego's plan for our salvation then involved casting our guilt outward into a fragmented universe in which we could both hide from God's wrath and act out our fantasy of autonomy by projecting that repressed but continually resurfacing guilt onto others in a perpetual cycle of attack and defense: a cycle intended to prove our relative innocence compared to another's greater sin.

The world is nothing in itself. Your mind must give it meaning. And what you behold upon it are your wishes, acted out so you can look on them and think them real.

Our wish to blame others for our loss of peace of mind, while avoiding responsibility for the original "crime" of separation, keeps a world of conflict, opposites, and opposition spinning. It also keeps us so busy fighting imaginary battles seemingly "out there" that we forget we have a decision maker in our mind that chose for the ego but can always choose again for the memory of wholeness, the reflection of the eternal, pure, united love we never left symbolized by the Holy Spirit.

A Course in Miracles teaches us to recognize our mistaken perception by catching ourselves in the act of holding others responsible for our suffering and realizing that we have chosen to suffer because it at least proves our individuality real. As we learn to practice forgiveness *A Course in Miracles* style, recognizing our projections as mere attempts to get rid of the painful guilt in our mind, taking them back to our mind and choosing again for the Holy Spirit's truth we never really left, our one mind begins to heal. In this way, the Holy Spirit offers the antidote to our mistaken perception. How? By using the very projections the ego invented to prevent the memory of the one true love we are from resurfacing in our minds to *undo* our error. Applying forgiveness in our relationships over time we gradually awaken from a dream that can at best offer only fleeting pleasure, and always ends in the body's death, the ultimate unfair treatment.

Perhaps you think you did not make the world, but came unwillingly to what was made already, hardly waiting for your thoughts to give it meaning. Yet in truth you found exactly what you looked for when you came.

The world we think we navigate always delivers exactly what the mind on ego has secretly asked for, proof of our martyrdom at another's hands; tampered-with evidence designed to convince a vengeful, dualistic God created by the ego in its own image that we should go to heaven, while those who wronged us go to hell. But we are already living a hell of our own making, the hell of conflict and competing interests we call this world. The good news?

> There is no world! This is the one central thought the Course attempts to teach...And if it is indeed your own imagining, then you can loose it from all things you ever thought it was by merely changing all the thoughts that gave it these appearances...To free the world from every kind of pain is but to change your mind about yourself.

To free ourselves we need but change our mind about the world. That means we first need to see it clearly for the defense against truth it is. We begin by tuning in to the 24/7 broadcast of our projected judgment and recognizing it for the moving, morphing external image of an internal state it represents. We will never find peace and happiness in a world designed to conceal the murderous thought of separation from eternal, whole love. Searching for salvation in such a world will never work. But recognizing our attraction to keeping a world of separation intact, realizing how much pain our mistaken judgments cost us, and choosing to release our erroneous interpretation to the memory of wholeness we share, our one mind begins to heal and an earth intent on irreconcilable differences seems both less awesome and less threatening. We experience release and relief from the enervating attack/defense cycle that keeps this world and its soundtrack of sin, guilt, and fear spinning, and return to truth.

I who remain as God created me would loose the world from all I thought it was. For I am real because the world is not, and I would know my own reality.

Forgiving the Unforgivable

In a startling turn of events, my 16-year-old daughter invited me to chaperone a field trip with her IB history class.

"Who are you and what have you done with my real daughter?" I asked.

"Funny."

"Do I get to talk to your friends? Do I get to talk to your teacher? Do I get to ride the bus and bring a sack lunch?"

"Don't push your luck, Mom," she said.

Of course I was secretly thrilled. And I got to do all of the above. Still, in my haste to bond with my daughter and her world, I hadn't even bothered to ask where we were going. Turns out, we were headed for a new museum in downtown Denver called The Cell (Center for Empowered Living and Learning) and its debut exhibit: "Anyone, Anytime, Anywhere: Understanding the Threat of Terrorism." The exhibit purports to "explore the many facets of terrorism, its threats and impact on the lives of people in Denver, the United States, and around the world."

The teacher had assigned students particular questions to consider based on interactive, multimedia displays. As at the Spy Museum in Washington, DC, you assume the identity of a real person (in this case a terrorist or victim) as you enter and discover your fate at the end. Out of fifty-six students, only a handful survived. But as chaperone, I was there to merely observe, keep the kids out of trouble, answer the occasional question, and consider my own questionable identity in relation to the continual stream of frightened voices and horrific flashing images of civilians being taken out by people all over the world intent on martyring themselves for the "greater good;" an extreme demonstration of the ego thought system's madness.

The students surveyed a wide array of innovative weapons crafted from ordinary objects used to accomplish violent acts. Small TVs streamed children's programs created to coerce young kids into joining the cause. People in a lovely anonymous town square sipped coffee at outdoor cafes, bought flowers, and rode their bikes before a backpack bomber put an end to an otherwise idyllic autumn afternoon. Another exhibit offered clues to the labyrinth of terrorist funding sources. On one wall, in excruciating slow motion, the twin towers crumbled, rose, and crumbled again. Talking heads from Homeland Security advocated staying alert to the signs of terrorism and preached steps we can all take to recognize and report suspicious activity.

"Why do they hate us so much?" one student asked. "Maybe because they're poor," another answered. But she sounded doubtful. The exhibit not only provided no real answers; it did not even embrace the most obvious question. But it seems to me *A Course in Miracles* provides the answer. The mind on ego we all share carries a brutal burden of unconscious guilt over the mistaken belief that it not only separated from its source but destroyed the kingdom on the way out the door. According to the ego's insane, albeit unconscious, scenario, God will nonetheless rise from the dead to punish us unless we can convince him we are innocent victims of another. Intent on proving our bogus individuality no matter the cost, we reenact that original thought of murder on an individual level and on a collective, cultural level; hell-bent on pinning our unconscious guilt over having severed perfect, unified love on someone else to demonstrate our relative innocence. *A Course in Miracles* trains us to bring the problem we perceive outside ourselves back to its source/cause in the mind. When we recognize it as another example of the one mind's projected guilt and choose again for the part of our mind that recognizes the unreality of the cause of our attack, we experience a shift in perception, a change of mind that holds no one prisoner.

On the level of form, however, when confronted by the ego gone mad on a nauseatingly massive scale, I find myself severely challenged to practice the Course's forgiveness. The process of recognizing the reflected guilt in my projection, taking back responsibility for my mistaken interpretation and asking for another interpretation from my right mind can seem impossible in such circumstances. But when I break it down, when I look at it with my inner teacher display by display, frame by frame, I am able to see that we all experience the same miserable impulse toward martyrdom in our relationships.

Of course, I, Susan, the false self I still think I am, did not cause these terrorist attacks. But the cause lies in the mind and the Course tells us again and again there is only one mind on the level of truth—one mind that believes it destroyed God to claim its independence; one mind crippled by the burden of that guilt; one mind intent on projecting it on someone else; one tortured mind that has nothing to do with a body's brain. The Course also tells us over and over that the life we believe we experience through our bodies is not real. We have imprisoned ourselves in a dream of our own making designed to protect us from punishment while preserving the impossible notion of individuality. The Course's forgiveness, then, always begins with the reminder that we are forgiving what never really happened. As we learn in Part II of the workbook's questions and answers, under What is Forgiveness?:

Forgiveness recognizes what you thought your brother did to you has not occurred. It does not pardon sins and make them real. It sees there was no sin. And in that view are all your sins forgiven.

With help from the part of our mind that does not believe in the horror of human experience but remembers only the one love we keep pushing away in our fear, we recognize that at some point we all feel misunderstood, misrepresented, unfairly treated; financially and psychologically exploited. We all indoctrinate our children in a history of our particular individual, family and cultural suffering. The ego thought system was hard-wired from the beginning to reflect irreconcilable differences. Believing it launched the most horrible of all attacks in the first place it continues to compulsively attack and defend. We cannot escape from or fix this vicious cycle of attack and defense by acting within it. We can only heal the cycle by first accepting the healing of our one mind. And because minds are joined unless I include you in my healing, I remain in perpetual combat in the dream and unable to awaken to truth.

"There must be another way," psychologist Bill Thetford told his colleague, Course scribe Helen Schuman, more than forty years ago. Forgiveness *A Course in Miracles* style is that better way, the loving answer to Bill's plea for healing the conflict in his relationships. Workbook lesson 134, "Let me perceive forgiveness as it is," contrasts the world's view of forgiveness with the Course's version. According to the world's version, what the Course refers to as "forgiveness to destroy," I enhance my ego by taking the high road in forgiving your heinous attack. This strengthens and perpetuates the ego's story of persecution designed to conceal its unconscious guilt over separating from its source by projecting/blaming it on someone/thing "outside." Thus, I avoid all responsibility for my state of mind. I am the innocent victim I tell myself and everyone else I can convince to listen (hopefully including God); secretly rejoicing in every seeming affront that once again proves my relative virtue. But even though I have been clearly wronged, I will forgive what you have done because that's just the kind of saintly ego I am.

Forgiveness to destroy protects my projection while celebrating my benevolence. The problem? It never works for long. The underlying guilt in my mind remains unscathed as the weary world winds on, constantly resurfacing and demanding I once more perceive myself unfairly treated to reestablish my innocence at another's expense.

Forgiveness *A Course in Miracles* style, au contraire, *undoes* my guilt over a sin that never happened by returning my judgment of you to the decision maker in my mind and inviting another interpretation of my skewed perception. It releases my repressed guilt over my desire to experience autonomy in exchange for eternal love/wholeness. Over time, practicing forgiveness by recognizing my projections and their secret purpose, observing my identification with the ego thought system, and actively choosing again for the part of my mind that remembers our original state of infinite oneness, my belief in competing interests wanes along with my addiction to individuality and I begin to awaken to the peace of our true, non-dualistic nature. The Course's forgiveness has given my life new meaning and real purpose: the healing of my split mind.

When I, the decision maker, choose the Holy Spirit as my teacher instead of the ego, I can perceive the terrorism of the ego's thought system without believing in it. But first I must look at my investment in the ego's version of forgiveness that has kept the attack/defense cycle in play; the peace I have traded to preserve a false identity that has only brought me pain, preventing me from experiencing the one love we are and have never left; a non-specific, abstract love beyond our current understanding we can nonetheless recall when we choose a different vision of the world that seems to spin with such drama, purpose, conflict and, ultimately, terror.

Forgiveness requires us to honestly look at the world we have created to both hide and reinforce our secret wish to live as individuals at God's expense, our fear of punishment, and our continuing reluctance to awaken from the ego's dream of denial we have accepted as our earthly reality. What motivates us to change? Bringing our projections back to the light of our one right mind where the memory of perfect wholeness has never stopped shining and thereby experiencing the deep comfort of our true nature.

But how do we forgive the unforgivable? How do we find common ground with those who seem wholly evil? To forgive those responsible for human atrocities given the traditional definition of forgiveness would be pure folly. But forgiving under the Course's definition always first recognizes we are forgiving the *unreal* illusion of guilt in the mind. It also recognizes what happens on the level of truth when the murderous thought of original separation is taken to its extreme. Terrorists feel wholly justified in martyrdom that proves their greater innocence versus their enemies' greater guilt, with an ego-invented, vengeful God as their witness.

It helps to look at my desire to distance myself from so-called "inhuman acts" with the gentle help of our loving inner teacher that reminds me that deeply buried beneath the appearance of mass murder I would condemn lies the desire to push the love of God, the one love we are, away—a desire shared by all the seemingly separated ones. I have moments (the Course calls them "holy instants") in which the Holy Spirit's interpretation dawns on my mind and I am healed, but most of the time, I still want to draw lines in the sand between the forgivable and the unforgivable. But the Course's form of forgiveness is a journey in undoing all my illusions, the path I have chosen to lead me home. And so I once more turn my judgment over, hoping as Jesus tells us again and again that our awakened mind is "so close to you we cannot fail."

Ultimately, I forgive and forgive again because I am learning to accept that I can't make it home without you and I want to go home more than I want to continue to play in a dream gone bad. Minds are joined because there is still only one mind, despite our hallucinated reality show of dueling personalities, viewpoints, and special interests. Heavily fortified by the vision of the Holy

Spirit, I learn to look beyond even the most horrific demonstrations of the ego's mantra of "kill or be killed," to recognize them as reflections of the one mind's denied guilt over a crime that *never occurred*, and to exchange them for the state of united, uninterrupted innocence we remain—a state I finally realize I want more than I want this autonomous self, always seeking to triumph at someone else's expense.

I did not make this up. Practicing forgiveness helps me realize that siding with this special self keeps me on a roller coaster of painful conflict relieved only by moments of fleeting happiness, while choosing for wholeness brings stability and deep comfort. We go home together or not at all, as this beautiful section from The Lifting of the Veil at the conclusion of Chapter 19's The Obstacles to Peace reminds us:

> This brother who stands beside you still seems to be a stranger. You do not know him, and your interpretation of him is very fearful. And you attack him still, to keep what seems to be yourself unharmed. Yet in his hands is your salvation. You see his madness, which you hate because you share it. And all the pity and forgiveness that would heal it gives way to fear. Brother, you need forgiveness of your brother, for you will share in madness or in Heaven together. And you and he will raise your eyes in faith together or not at all.

Recalculating Forgiveness

It has been a slow few days here on the forgiveness front, a little lull in the attack-defense cycle during which I have reveled in actually reading the Course again while the ego cooks up its next oral argument for some thing or one "out there" intent on destroying or enhancing the self I consistently forget I am not. In the meantime, I am savoring *A Course in Miracles* workbook lesson 71: "Only God's plan for salvation will work," and considering the idea that we have a direction in this life, some preordained destination: destiny, fate, call it what you will; the idea that the self I think I am has somewhere *special* to go, some *special* plan to fulfill, some grand, *special* scheme in which to fit, my *special* piece in the puzzle of the universe to deliver; that tiny mad idea.

I am thinking about the tantalizing (to the ego) idea that we have a direction in this seeming life, and how I have spent a good deal of my time on this planet both figuratively and literally in the driver's seat of a vehicle getting lost, frantically worrying about getting lost and secretly rejoicing in getting lost. Although I pride myself on an intuitive sense of direction that has helped me navigate ancient European cities and the warren-like back streets of medieval Italian hill towns on foot, I have been known to disappear for hours on straight country roads in Colorado. Desolate stretches interrupted only by bobble-headed prairie dogs and imaginary, lunging *Indiana Jones*-scaled rattlesnakes whizzing by in my peripheral vision.

When I lived in California, in those pioneering days before cell phones, I would head out on the highway to interview someone outside city limits only to end up hours later feeding dimes into a phone booth while struggling to get my bearings from a set of oil rigs perched like grazing dinosaurs on a bald hillside somewhere in that great valley that still supplies most of our nation with year-round produce. (*Wherever,* I came to think of it, in true Valley Girl vernacular.) I attracted similarly handicapped companions. My friend Beth and I once headed out of town to a yoga retreat in the Sonoma Valley—a reward for another successful bout of quitting smoking—and ended up somewhere outside Sacramento, after following a sign to a stand selling almond-stuffed olives we just had to try. (A wrong turn we only discovered when run off the road by a trucker, rudely interrupting another of our scintillating conversations.)

But I digress the way I do. I am thinking about the idea of

getting lost and not getting lost and the many forgiveness opportunities it has offered me in my marriage of nearly twenty years. My husband is a man who believes in maps. I am a woman who believes in following my muse and, when she fails as she inevitably does, driving until I find a gas station and someone to ask. Maps have a purpose, of course. Early American and old European versions make frame-worthy art. But, although I am perfectly capable of reading them, I find doing so at best a terrible distraction and at worst, a life-threatening obsession. In a driver's seat, the map-dependent sacrifice safety in their fixation with arriving at a pre-ordained destination, struggling to unfold, read, and re-fold said maps while balancing a steering wheel between their knees, refusing to listen to verbal directions from well meaning passengers. They do not speak the language of "left and right" and "probably just around that bend" with which I am content and fluent. Even on a hike, the map-dependent will stop every few yards on clearly marked trails to verify their location like newly arrived aliens, driving their map-adverse spouses to constantly climb and return, climb and return, like loyal, albeit bored-to-tears, dogs.

But I digress the way I do, on roads and trails and on the page. Enter the handy little device that has transformed our family's road trips over the last couple years: the Garmin GPS portable navigation system, a gadget I resisted but have come to embrace as a metaphor for releasing to the Holy Spirit my belief that I know where I am going on any level. For those of you unfamiliar with the wonders of this contraption, you attach it to your windshield and type in the address of your destination. You select a voice from an array of international male and female possibilities (my favorite is a Brit who sounds like the actor Colin Firth but my husband prefers a woman with a French accent we call Fifi) and off you go. The device offers those of us with auditory preferences the verbal cues we crave to prevent interrupting our ruminations on passing views, while appeasing the map-dependent with a depiction of their vehicle traversing the route on a tiny screen, the opportunity to star in some kind of twisted, virtual road trip game.

Although I admit I initially met the introduction of this latest toy into our vehicle with a fair amount of skepticism, I eventually recognized its value on a symbolic level and have come to—if not entirely revere forfeiting control of my journey—at least understand that I may be better off deferring to an outside guide privy to information I do not have. Like the right mind, *A Course in Miracles* constantly encourages us (the decision maker) to choose for, our Garmin knows things about where we are going we do not, and would never lead us astray. On purpose, anyway.

This is far from a perfect analogy, of course, because there are times when the Garmin is wrong, a victim of mistaken programming. The Holy Spirit on the other hand is never wrong, and, unlike the ego, never the victim of anything. The Holy Spirit in our mind holds the memory of our true direction: returning home to the one, indivisible love we never left by awakening from this dream of separation. Still, I have come to admire the Garmin's manner in patiently leading us back when we have once again deluded ourselves we know better. Should we fail to take its advice, it never scolds but simply tries to follow our latest mistake in the dream, to make itself once more available. "Recalculating," it says, scanning to find us where we think we are in this world headed nowhere, and adjusting the route accordingly until we choose again for the path that will take us home.

All destinations I have sought and continue to seek in this world reflect my wish to make the ego's plan for salvation real. The plan depends on always seeking outside myself for some person, place, or thing to make me whole: an impossible plan designed to fail us.

According to this insane plan, any perceived source of

salvation is acceptable provided that it will not work. This ensures that the fruitless search will continue, for the illusion persists that, although this hope has always failed, there is still grounds for hope in other places and in other things.

Despite their celebrated differences, the map-dependent and the map-adverse both blindly follow the ego's plan of seek but do not find, always hoping the next destination will deliver the thrill of a lifetime and only becoming more and more lost in an illusory world.

For what could more surely guarantee that you will not find salvation than to channelize all your efforts in searching for it where it is not?

The ego cherishes both the notion that it knows where it is going, and the secret, denied desire to become hopelessly lost in an external, combative reality designed to keep it permanently unaware that it has a mind able to choose again for the Holy Spirit.

Like the Garmin, the Holy Spirit in our mind knows things we do not; like where we think we left and where we're really going. It doesn't beat us over the head with this information but, like our handy little Garmin, waits for us to ask and then suggests another way. Like the Garmin, the Holy Spirit encourages us to catch ourselves when we have run amuck, to recognize our error could not have occurred outside the mind in a hallucinated world, and to recalculate, returning the error to the source of the mistake in the mind and choosing again for a corrected route home—the only place we really want to go.

For the Love of God

As a child, I would sit in church trying to feel God's love. From what I had gleaned so far, hell and our church of the Immaculate

Conception shared a lot of common attributes. Both were temperature-challenged, for example. In winter, the furnace clanked and wheezed like a train anxious to pull away from the station as we sat sweltering in our winter coats atoning for our many transgressions. In summer sweat on the priests' foreheads rained into the communion chalice and stained the armpits of grownups' garments. Like the inferno I feared spending eternity in if I didn't manage to pull myself together, church stank from all that comingled incense, sweat, and guilt. People suffered there, the living, breathing variety as well as the ornamental: from a statue of Mary mashing a snake with her bare feet—which, despite her beatific expression could not have felt good—to Jesus nailed to a cross above the altar, crowned with thorns, bleeding for our sins, and peering down at us with beseeching eyes I could never bring myself to meet.

As a child, I would sit in church trying to feel God's love despite its similarities to our Catechism's hell. Sometimes I thought I felt it for a moment, on my knees, fist to heart, transported by the rhythm of a Latin phrase. More often I only felt the rage rising in me again at the injustice of my brother fiddling with the hymnal beside me, swinging his feet, making those little sucking noises by drawing spit through the hole where his front teeth used to be. Our mother staring straight ahead between us, her fingers closing hand-cuff like on both our wrists as if I, too, were ultimately headed for the slammer.

He was wearing that stupid clip-on bowtie; my brother, making that face like Stan Laurel in *Laurel and Hardy* in his efforts to cajole our father into cracking a smile, our mother to cut off our circulation. I was not a bad child, all things considered, even saintly at times, but who could expect any reasonable person to feel the love of God through the haze of such completely justifiable hatred?

I have been thinking about the early years I spent trying to feel the love of God sitting on a hard pew in a hot church surrounded by my family, and the decades that followed searching for that elusive condition in one venue after another, obediently following the ego's orders of "seek but do not find." Only recently—nearly six years into practicing *A Course in Miracles*—have I begun to glimpse that what I am seeking cannot exist outside my mind. Although I still catch myself craving the external form of what passes for love in this world, I have trained my mind to recognize my mistake as it arises from moment to moment, and, in so doing, begun to understand, accept and allow my only purpose in this dream: healing my mind about where love really resides—and thereby experiencing it again. As Chapter 30's The Only Purpose puts it:

The real world is the state of mind in which the only purpose of the world is seen to be forgiveness...The value of forgiveness is perceived and takes the place of idols, which are sought no longer, for their 'gifts' are not held dear. No rules are idly set, and no demands are made of anyone or anything to twist and fit into the dream of fear. Instead, there is a wish to understand all things created as they really are. And it is recognized that all things must be first forgiven, and then understood.

This latter statement echoes *A Course in Miracles* early workbook lessons that invite us to suspend our disbelief and embrace the possibility that nothing we experience, none of the information our senses so obediently transmit to the ego's brain, has anything to do with our true nature. Our experience in the world of form can never deliver the love we continually seek, fleetingly find, and forfeit again and again in this trippy dream of exile we continue to feed to prove our uniqueness. We must learn to allow the undoing of *all* we know to experience fear's opposite, the indivisible, eternal love we remain. We must allow forgiveness to precede understanding.

Lately, as I practice forgiveness, allowing that old mistaken rage at my brother for keeping me from winning God's love to surface and asking for help from the part of my mind that knows we remain one despite the seeming solidity of attacking figures in the dream, an acute awareness of my buried desire to push away God's love, the one love we are, has also surfaced. I am noticing—as I go through my days, allowing people and events to either enhance or diminish the self I think I am—something interesting about what I really want. Even when love's reflection genuinely arises, even when my husband or daughter extends the one love we are to me in the holy instant, I often turn away. Real love, love you can count on, the eternal, whole, unalterable, unconditional variety we have never left but secretly believe we destroyed, still scares the hell out of me! That is where I am at this moment in my journey home. Even though the part of me that always watches now, the decision maker in my mind, is learning from experience that it will feel better if it chooses again for truth I continue at times to choose for pain by turning away from the presence of love that forever lingers in our mind.

I believe in the Course's radical form of forgiveness; I have experienced its benefits; I continue to teach it, to learn, and yet I am still at times unwilling to forgive myself for my reluctance to allow the peace my whole mind offers. Sometimes, I am still that little girl on her knees in church beating her chest and wishing she could instead use her fist on the kid beside her who actually deserves it. I still at times oscillate between blaming others and blaming myself for a crime that never really happened. That's how afraid I am of disappearing into the void. That's how convincing and appealing this individual body still seems, navigating a world it believes means something, a world in which having loved and fought, won and lost, lived and died, *means* something.

A Course in Miracles does not ask us to look at how loving we are. Instead it asks us to notice how unloved and unloving our thoughts, how ultimately futile our efforts to find stable, permanent peace in an unstable, impermanent thought system that arose from the unstable, impermanent idea of separation. Fortunately, the Course offers us an internal guide that meets us where we think we are in this illusion: a guide that knows our every fear but also knows we have nothing to fear; a guide that remembers what never happened, and what has always been.

The author of *A Course in Miracles* knows we, in bodies, can't believe this by ourselves. It speaks to us as a loving older sibling to a small child writhing in her bed, enduring a nightmare, on her knees and beating her chest to stave off the punishment she has coming for her murderous thoughts toward her brother. Our inner teacher metaphorically rests his hand on our feverish forehead, quieting our torment, whispering to us from outside the dream that we are, have always been and forever remain safe, whole, loved and loving, despite the erroneous information our senses continue to propagate. Resting to the music of our guide's voice our trust in forgiveness strengthens, our horrific nightmare gradually morphs into a peaceful dream, and we inch a little closer to opening our eyes for good.

My Mind Is Preoccupied with Past Thoughts

Our new puppy, Kayleigh, had been whimpering in her crate off and on all night. She normally cried a few minutes after I put her to bed before settling down but we had only adopted her a week-and-a-half ago and "normal" was still a moving target. All the experienced dog owners I talked to swore by enforcing the crating routine and so I tossed and turned all night, awakening to her soft cries, alternating between annoyance and worry, fighting an overwhelming urge to liberate her.

At four-thirty I'd had enough. Without turning on the light, I swaddled her in a towel and took her back to bed with me. Deep sighs shuddered through her tiny frame. I held her tighter as she burrowed into the folds of the towel before finally falling asleep.

We lay like that a long time waiting for the delayed autumn sunrise, a week short of setting our clocks back. Finally, in the milky light of dawn, I discovered the cause of her upset. She had soiled her crate, clearly a victim of some kind of intestinal distress. She gazed at me with sad eyes, trembling as I tried to comfort her, issuing those same forlorn sighs I now recognized as a mantra of canine shame.

Guilt over failing to rescue her earlier washed over me as I called the vet to get her in that morning and cleaned up after her new accidents, all the while trying to reassure her that she was just sick, not a bad dog; it would be OK. I had recently started *A Course in Miracles* workbook again with a class I was teaching and attempted to focus on today's workbook lesson 8: "My mind is preoccupied with past thoughts," but couldn't really concentrate, distraught over our puppy's state and distracted with regret over having left her all night sick and alone.

At the vet's she lay listless in my arms as the nurse explained they would test for several infections and make sure the distemper inoculation series she had not yet completed had delivered the necessary protection. When they carried her off to perform required tortures behind stainless steel doors, tears sprang to my eyes. I mentally admonished myself to get a grip. This was not a child after all, but a puppy I had known for less than two weeks and yet she weighed less than two pounds and had already become my adoring shadow; dependent on me for her every need; wholly trusting in my good intentions.

The nurse returned with the vet. The good news? They had eliminated the most serious possibility and hoped the lab work would deliver more information in a day or two. The bad? Kayleigh was seriously dehydrated. It doesn't take much for a dog closer in size to a hamster to deplete itself. They would need to start her on an IV. With any luck, I could pick her up about 7 p.m.

As they whisked her away, I wandered out to my car struggling to keep from sobbing, plagued by the thought that she might die on a cold table among strangers. Driving home, memories of my daughter's hospitalization for a serious bout of pneumonia at three months old came boomeranging back. Sixteen years ago, I had been so numb and clueless in the emergency room, insisting on holding my infant through every procedure save for the X-ray during which her screams pierced my heart. As a young, frightened mother I don't think I actually allowed myself to entertain the possibility of losing her over the three-week ordeal that ensued. But Kayleigh's precarious state seemed to have resurrected that long passed possibility. I drove home in a fog of emotion completely forgetting about *A Course in Miracles*, the classroom of my life, and the value of applying the content of the workbook lessons to my current curriculum.

Worried and distracted, I showered, alternating between trying to check in with my right mind and focusing on a work project, before calling to check on Kayleigh. She had eaten and gotten feisty, even chewed through her IV. "That's my girl," I thought. The phone rang. It was my human daughter this time, crying with such conviction I could not make out a word she said. I steadied my voice even as my stomach turned over in fear.

I talked to her for a few minutes faking that same, sure, calm Mama voice I used with the dog until the bad news gurgled forth. She had gone to a study session at a nearby coffee house on her off period and gotten a speeding ticket on her way back to school. Remorseful and terrified of her father's reaction, as well as having to appear in court, stressed out from midterms, and still suffering a severe sore throat despite having just finished a round of antibiotics for Strep, she spun out of emotional control. I continued to talk her down until I felt she could drive home. It would be OK, I told her. It was a bad mistake and a big lesson that would have consequences, but fortunately no one had been hurt. We would talk about it.

As I waited for her to drive home from school, I tried to

become still enough to access my right mind and return to the workbook lesson but could not shake my worry over my daughter and puppy or the all too familiar urge to blame someone or thing for my downwardly spiraling mental state. Nothing that had happened since I closed the door on Kayleigh's crate the night before had complied with a single plan I had made. Instead, I found myself reluctantly fielding an unrelenting series of expertly pitched curveballs. Actually, the entire week had fallen far short of expectations, the ego quickly pointed out. My writing projects had been severely disrupted by the rigors of caring for a new puppy, the house was a mess, and the novel I had finally finished and started querying agents about had so far only elicited rejection. An organization with which I was involved continued to take a philosophic turn with which I disagreed, my back was out again, and now my puppy's life hung by a thread and my daughter had broken the law. Before I could turn away from the ego's increasingly dramatic arguments and invite the voice of reason, my daughter walked in.

I brewed tea and spoke with her calmly, as the ego mind also activated in her presented its tragic case. She did not try to defend her behavior but did offer a coherent explanation for why she decided to exceed the speed limit to pass a truck carrying loose lumber and other debris she feared might fall out and hit her. In a raspy voice, she also expressed the stress she was under at school and the fear that certain friends had inexplicably turned their backs on her. After offering lots of reassurance about the nature of school and friends, and discussing the possible conse-quences for the ticket, I felt her forehead, peered into her throat, and decided she, too, should see a doctor.

Impersonating Supermom, while also internally complaining that this seriously had to be one of the worst days in recent memory, we drove to Kaiser Medical Center to learn she still had Strep, picked up another round of antibiotics, and rushed to the vet's to pick up the dog, prescription food and medicine. Driving home, as the front pushing in a much publicized pre-season snowstorm descended, I phoned my husband to see if he would stop for some plain yogurt with active cultures the vet had recommended for Kayleigh. When he later appeared swinging a six-pack of flavored yogurt with added vitamins and fiber, my fragile grip on reality further relaxed. I am sorry to say the ego pounced. Why couldn't he ever *listen* to me?

"I asked for plain yogurt," I said.

"It's just vanilla."

"She's a puppy. She can't have flavored yogurt. She can't have sugar and extra fiber." What was not to get about this?

"You want me to throw it out? You want me to take it back?"

I turned away. We had been here before.

Licking my imaginary wounds, I carried our puppy upstairs, got ready for bed, put her back in her crate, and listened for the dreaded crying but the exhausted animal had instantly fallen asleep. I, on the other hand, lay awake reviewing my frustration with the series of events that seemed to have hijacked not only the day but all shreds of my fragile connection with inner peace. The title phrase of the day's workbook lesson, the words that had been eluding me all day, at last returned: "My mind is preoccupied with past thoughts."

I recalled sitting at the vet's that morning, waiting for them to return with my puppy, sitting in the emergency room all those years ago waiting for them to finish X-raying my screaming baby. I recalled waiting for an array of bodily test results over the years, waiting for people to die, waiting for clients to get back to me, waiting for agents and publishers to accept or reject my writing, affirm or destroy my self-worth, waiting for my daughter or husband to call to let me know they had arrived at their destination safely, waiting and waiting and waiting for them to comply with my requests. Waiting, waiting, waiting; preoccupied with past thoughts.

The one wholly true thought one can hold about the past is

that it is not here.

This sounds sophomoric, on the surface, taken literally. But when understood, according to *A Course in Miracle's* revelatory thought system, when taken on the level of the truth we are, the truth the Course teaches us abides *outside* this dream of self-imposed exile, it offers an absolute, albeit slippery, reality we who believe we reside in differentiated bodies find almost impossible to grasp. The one, whole truth we are resides in the eternal present, the non-dualistic, indivisible love without beginning or end we believe we shattered in exchange for a differentiated, traumatic past and a future of competing interests and derailed days. The present completely eludes the ego because in its eternal wholeness the finite, illusory ego disappears. The present means death to the ego, death to the individuality we fight so valiantly to protect at the cost of infinite, invulnerable, sanity. As we go about our days reacting on the basis of our past traumas or triumphs and anticipating something better or worse we unconsciously preserve and reinforce the ego thought system, mindlessly projecting our underlying guilt over turning our backs on our one wholly loved and loving self onto someone or thing "outside."

> Very few have realized what is actually entailed in picturing the past or in anticipating the future. The mind is actually blank when it does this, because it is not really thinking about anything.

All day, as I "endured" the problems seemingly confronting me out of nowhere, I completely forgot I am the dreamer of this dream, responsible for inventing its characters and plotline, for writing yet another fiction to convince myself I am a living, breathing, individual interacting with other living, breathing individuals; trying to solve an array of random problems the part of our one mind that took the tiny mad idea of separation seriously specifically created to keep us from ever getting back to the decision maker in our one mind; that part of our one mind capable of watching the ego's theatrics, recognizing them for yet another defense against truth, and choosing again (even as we deal with them on the level of form) to gently smile at our mistake with the part of our mind that knows it's only a dream.

Recognizing that your mind has been merely blank, rather than believing that it is filled with real ideas, is the first step to opening the way to vision.

As I lay listening to the soft rise and fall of our puppy's breath emanating from her crate on the floor, the day's frenzied, fearful drama receded and my judgments waned. All my past regrets, all my wishes and fears, dropped away in the stillness of our joined breath. Our breathing seemed to expand to envelop the whole sleeping world and for an elongated grateful moment, before I slipped from the waking into the sleeping dream within a dream, I paused between breaths, allowing myself to enter the eternal present we have never left, truly resting. Open, healed, and complete in God.

An Untrained Mind Can Accomplish Nothing

When I first started *A Course in Miracles'* workbook lessons six years ago, I have to admit my mind glazed over every time I opened the book. I could barely absorb the meaning of a single phrase before I started mentally making grocery lists, puzzling solutions to work projects, worrying about what my daughter was or was not doing, rehearsing a conversation I needed to have with a troubling colleague, reviewing the details of an argument I'd had with my husband, or slipping into an overwhelmingly sleepy trance.

I recently started the workbook lessons again with a class I am teaching and am amazed anew at how much these early lessons stir up the ego and bring me face to face with my ongoing resistance to the truth of what we are. I have done the first part of the workbook designed to undo the ego thought system maybe nine times, because I at least recognize that my investment in the ego needs undoing before I can even begin to fathom the revelatory, comforting messages of the second part.

A Course in Miracles invites us to begin to view our lives as a classroom, our experiences and relationships, as a curriculum, and the part of our mind that failed to take "the tiny mad idea" of separation seriously—that forgotten, sane part of our mind—as our new teacher. These early lessons meet us where we think we are here in the world of perception, ingeniously directing us to focus on and begin questioning the distracting information our senses transmit to our brains—the ego's "proof" that we pulled off the impossible and exist as separate entities. They remind us, for example, that nothing we see means anything, that we have given everything we see all the meaning that it has for us, that we are never upset for the reason we think, that we see only the past, and that our thoughts do not mean anything.

The ego recoils from these messages because they overlook its erroneous existence. If the ego mind does not exist, if nothing outside the one mind exists and the world and the body exist outside the mind, as A Course in Miracles claims, then I, Susan, the self I think I am with all my special needs and problems, talents and handicaps; do not, in truth, exist. No wonder our minds wander, we grow sleepy, and we can't remember the title of a lesson for more than thirty seconds. No wonder you don't see people stampeding to bookstores to pick up their very own copy of this big, blue book, but you do see people snapping up books teaching us how to manipulate, fix, improve, and attract in an illusory world of form. It's much easier to just keep denying our negative feelings, projecting them on others, and showing everyone how loving, happy, and spiritual we are. But it's an exhausting charade offering at best temporary fixes that never reach the root of the problem. At some point we exceed our tolerance for pain and pretense and cry out for a better way. *A Course in Miracles* offers it.

As Ken Wapnick enjoys reminding us, however, this is a teaching for spiritual infants. The exceedingly rare enlightened individual (I am told these people exist; it has not been my pleasure to actually meet one) has no need for this book. Those of us who believe in and value our individuality over the one, whole, indivisible love we have never in truth left on the other hand must first *unlearn* everything the ego has taught us before we can welcome the love of our true, non-dualistic nature.

We who believe in and value our separate physical and emotional bodies and personalities above truth have bought the ego's bizarre myth that we destroyed our eternal creator, deserve punishment, and must continually repress/deny responsibility for what we have done through the unconscious habit of blaming other people and situations for our problems. In this way, we magically hope to avoid the punishment we believe we deserve while simultaneously experiencing the rewards of playing here in the world of form. But no matter how much fun we may have on the playground, someone always gets hurt. No matter what a blast we have on the monkey bars, children always grow up, age, and eventually sicken, and die. This is what we've traded for eternal love, peace, wholeness and creativity. This is how deluded we are. This is why we need a workbook to *unlearn* what we have willingly taught ourselves in an effort to keep the one love we have come to fear away.

Our one mind has been so well trained by the ego it has completely forgotten it has a mind outside the waking dream of separation we call life. Love in our current state is literally beyond us. Enter the role of the Course's workbook lessons. As we learn in the workbook's introduction:

An untrained mind can accomplish nothing...The purpose of

the workbook is to train your mind in a systematic way to a different perception of everyone and everything in the world. The exercises are planned to help you generalize the lessons, so that you will understand that each of them is equally applicable to everyone and everything you see.

Every workbook lesson shines the same wise light on all our experiences, illuminating the truth that lies beyond our illusions. As we apply our learning to our experiences, we begin to see all our problems and difficulties—from minor annoyances to major catastrophes—as reflections of the only real problem: our belief that we could have separated from our indivisible source. We begin to spiritually mature and our split mind begins to heal. By learning to accept responsibility for our mistaken perception and observing it from the viewpoint of our enlightened inner teacher, our faith in the ego's lies erodes and we experience glimmers of the eternal light that lies beyond the façade we made to block our awareness of love's presence. As we learn to look with our inner teacher, to alter our perception of everyone and everything through the Course's forgiveness, our investment in the meaning and value of our singular identity slips away.

Despite our unconscious resistance, the workbook lessons work to correct our mistaken perception if we apply them. We all resist; we all forget; our minds wander and become preoccupied with meaningless thoughts. We grow distracted and sleepy. Sometimes we experience a full-blown ego attack, projecting all that bottled up fear and guilt on the first poor sucker to cross our path. Regardless of the form it takes, it helps to recognize resistance for the fear of love it represents, gently forgive ourselves for our mistaken perception as we would a terrified child, and return once again to the lesson for the day.

As the workbook introduction also points out:

Some of the ideas the workbook presents you will find hard to believe, and others may seem to be quite startling. This does not matter. You are merely asked to apply the ideas as you are directed to do. You are not asked to judge them at all. You are only asked to use them. It is their use that will give them meaning to you, and will show you that they are true.

The workbook lessons teach us that when we resign as our own teacher, when we turn away from the ego's 24/7 rant of competing interests and unfair treatment, the deeply comforting memory of completeness returns and we find ourselves in the miracle of the holy instant, the eternal present: the place outside time where we pause a moment before rejoining the infinite love we have never really left.

Of course, we grow frightened again of disappearing into the primordial broth the ego has taught us means death. We grow frightened again by the ego's fairy tale of a God intent on punishing us for running away from home. But as we journey through the workbook, applying the lessons to the content of our lives, with the help of our new inner teacher, our belief in the ego's lies weakens without any additional effort on our part. We need only suspend our disbelief and follow the lessons' lead.

Awakening Happens
(And happens, and happens, and happens...)
Over decades of spiritual searching, I have met a handful of people who claim to have awakened to the truth beyond the dream of separate interests, the lives we believe we are living in this world. Most have undergone spontaneous, dramatic shifts in awareness usually following a particularly traumatic experience, such as physically dying for a few moments or coming very close to death. Others reached a point of psychological suffering wherein the realization that they could choose instead to experience wholeness finally dawned on them. These people went on to share their awakening with others, motivated to bring

light to our darkness. But all too often they unwittingly fell asleep again. Hypnotized by the "specialness" of their experience, they began to use it to elevate themselves above the masses, behaving as if they were somehow more deserving of the one love we share, somehow able to heal those less advanced and evolved, better equipped to hear the voice of love, in possession of the "secret" balm for what ails our broken souls.

While there must be cases of this type of sudden, pure awakening in which the individual then *remains* awake in this world—"in it but not of it" and able to demonstrate the one love we never left—I have never personally encountered such an individual. But I have met many whose longing and searching for truth beyond the dream, whose internal determination to look honestly within has offered glimpses of our true nature, moments of clarity in which time and need vanishes replaced by wonder and the joy of certain unity, the welcome death of the ego. I, too, have increasingly experienced—most frequently as a direct result of practicing *A Course in Miracle's* forgiveness—these "holy instants," before returning once more to a tumultuous venue of challenging relationships, preoccupation with physical survival: temporary fulfillment and success followed by disappointment and broken promises.

Why can't whole, infinite love stay? Or, more accurately, why can't we stay in that moment of awakened communion with the love we are, reunited with our true and only self? *A Course in Miracles* is the only path I have studied that answers and transcends that question, leading us beyond it by first inviting us to question all we believe about ourselves, the realm in which we seem to engage, and everything that appears to happen *to us*. By admitting we do not know what we are, what we're doing, or why we're doing it, we begin to scrape away at the false self and world we created to hide our true, shared light.

Why would we fear awakening to that whole, eternally loving truth? Because we believe we destroyed it. The moment the "tiny mad idea" of experiencing autonomy arose in the one child of God's mind and we took it seriously, we experienced ourselves *outside* that mind, cast into darkness, convinced our seeming error in judgment had somehow obliterated our source. Overcome with guilt and terrified of retribution, we hungrily swallowed the ego's plan of eliminating our guilt by projecting it outward into a world of constantly fragmenting, evolving, competing and opposing forms. And to make sure we never remembered we could simply choose again not to believe, we repressed the memory of that initial choice to separate, figuratively fell asleep, and completely forgot the awakened, invulnerable, eternal reality, no idea, however misguided, could possibly threaten.

The heavy burden of that unconscious guilt and fear which surfaces in the guise of every negative emotion—anger, annoyance, frustration, depression, grief, impatience, etc.— weighs heavily on our hearts. So heavily we can't bear it for long, and must blame it on others, or experience its return in the form of an outside attack from which we compulsively protect/defend our now fragile, finite, *false* selves. We (the decision maker that chose to follow the ego) also believe our separate identities offer us something worth attempting to preserve. That our "specialness" purchased at the cost of the one, indivisible love we've forgotten is worth the price of an unreliable, ultimately deteriorating, unique life punctuated by moments of pleasure and eventually defeated by tragedy.

A Course in Miracles offers us a process for awakening from the nightmare of our mistaken belief; harnessing the very illusory forms the ego thought system uses to reinforce its tale of separation to *undo* our belief in it. Little by little, practicing the Course's unique form of forgiveness that invites the decision maker to catch itself in the act of projecting, recognize the external attack/problem as merely an expression of repressed internal guilt and choose again for the vision of the part of our mind that recognizes our illusions but does not take them seriously, our error is corrected. Little by little, day by day, as we begin to witness our mistaken belief that someone or thing "outside" can in any way enhance or disturb our peace of mind, and recognize the suffering that belief causes, the ego thought system begins to weaken.

Motivated by an increasing awareness of the pain our investment in separation has cost us, we choose again, and again for truth, experiencing moments of awakening more and more frequently. Eventually, practicing forgiveness, our reaction to the movie of the outside world that once seemed so attractive and repulsive begins to fade along with our judgments. Old grudges, what the Course calls "ancient hatreds," slip away and we feel more balanced, kind, and tolerant. Something our spouse once did that drove us up the wall no longer rankles. A wave of appreciation washes over us as we notice something beautiful about our child's spirit we had overlooked before. An understanding that we all share the same mistaken belief and the same longing to dispel it replaces the details of our secret suffering and compassion begins to eclipse our experience of unfairness.

The miracle, the change of mind forgiveness brings, happens over and over in our journey home, undoing our false beliefs and gently awakening us from the nightmare of competition with our source we have been reenacting in our relationships for so long. Awakening *A Course in Miracles* style is ordinary business, an accessible, practical process anyone can undertake by patiently learning to apply its simple teaching to every experience we seem to encounter in our daily lives, despite the ego's fear tactics and active resistance. We don't have to set our sights on awakening; it happens, and happens and happens as we practice forgiveness anywhere, anytime, with anything we believe we interact. As the introduction to the workbook (the Course's companion to the text that teaches us to apply its dynamic forgiveness process in our everyday lives) reassures us in conclusion:

Remember only this; you need not believe the ideas, you need not accept them, and you need not even welcome them. Some of them you may actively resist. None of this will matter, or decrease their efficacy.

To Do: Forgive

I am a planner, a list maker, a "To Do" list junkie. Like my mother and grandmother before me, I rejoice in crossing tasks off my list—to the point that if I've accomplished something not on that day's list I add it on just so I can cross it off again. *I know.* Oddly enough, I also have never actually gotten to the bottom of a given list before creating a new one with a fresh set of goals to attempt to achieve. I am drunk on the idea of achievement, a slave to the ego in my frantic pursuit of *doing* yet always falling somehow short; a situation that keeps me rushing back again and again into the ego's brutal ring.

But *A Course in Miracles* is teaching me a better way. I am learning to use my life as a classroom, the events that seemingly arise in my day to circumvent the possibility of ever getting through my coveted To Do list as the curriculum of forgiveness necessary for *undoing* my belief in this special identity with its unique problems to solve and tasks to complete. I awoke last week, for example, filled with ambition, adrenaline pumping, ready to tackle a hefty list of responsibilities:

-Set up interview
-Transcribe notes for newspaper article
-Work on website copy
-Prep for workbook class
-Yoga class
-Query agents
-Bids on gas fireplaces
-Pick up office supplies
-Drop health forms for daughters' school trip at doctor's

My list sat accumulating importance on the bathroom counter where I leave it to greet me on awakening. I took our puppy out of her crate but before I could get her to follow me downstairs to take her outside, she had an accident on the rug. The difficult task of housebreaking any dog has been exacerbated in her case by a nasty bout of Giardia that had scared us badly and left her severely dehydrated and on an IV just two weeks ago. But she had finished a second round of antibiotics and appeared to be on the mend—at least, until now.

No need to share the gory details. Suffice it to say, the puppy was sicker this time than ever. My husband and I took turns dealing with her and showering. I threw the towels and rug she had soiled in the wash and tried to console her. She shuddered in shame over her loss of control as I wrapped her in a fresh towel. I sat rocking her in my office. I was teaching *A Course in Miracles'* workbook again and managed to read that morning's lesson 25: "I do not know what anything is for," answer a couple of emails and wolf down an English muffin before I reached the vet when they opened at nine.

Kayleigh and I waited in one of the examination rooms that had become all too familiar in our few weeks together. A nurse whisked her off for tests. I had taken some copy to edit but Kayleigh's weak screams, as they poked and prodded in a back room, blurred my vision. The nurse returned her to my lap and explained they were running more lab work. Kayleigh lay draped across my forearm. From the back room, the cries of a much larger dog—a shepherd or lab, maybe—pierced the stillness. It went on and on. Kayleigh cocked her head and gazed up at me, eyes filled with the other dog's misery, as if beseeching me to intervene. "It's OK," I lied. She buried her snout in the crux of my elbow.

At last, the doctor returned. Kayleigh had once again tested positive for Giardia, so positive they worried she might have contracted a drug-resistant strain. They were putting her on a couple medications to help treat the symptoms of her intestinal distress and put a call in to an organization that sounded like the animal version of The Centers for Disease Control for advice on what to do next. They would call me later that day. For the second time in two weeks, the fear of losing this animal I had so quickly come to adore washed over me.

I filled Kayleigh's prescription, picked up more of the special diet, and drove home in a fog of concern. Once again in my office after almost three hours, I sat back down at the computer, Kayleigh in my lap. The "To Do" list imprinted in my ego brain beckoned, but words from the morning's workbook lesson called more strongly. "I do not know what anything is for."

> You perceive the world and everything in it as meaningful in terms of ego goals. These goals have nothing to do with your own best interests, because the ego is not you. This false identity makes you incapable of understanding what anything is for.

The self I think I am, Susan sitting here with this tiny dog, Kayleigh, has only one interest when informed by the ego: reinforcing the belief in that original separation that seemed to occur when the one mind forgot to laugh at the "tiny mad idea" of striking off on its own; appearing to fragment the one, whole, indivisible, eternal love we are and, in truth, remain; a love that has nothing to do with the specifics of my personal interests, goals and accomplishments. Beginning to see the secret, mistaken purpose of those personal interests, goals and accomplishments from the viewpoint of the Holy Spirit—the part of my mind that recognizes my illusions but does not take them seriously—is what the Course calls "forgiveness," the only real goal I have in this world if I truly want (as I am learning I do) to awaken from this dream of exile from love.

While my work on the level where I think I reside has relative importance, and needs to command some of my attention while I operate here in a body on the level of form, I must learn to recognize it ultimately has no meaning on the level of truth. Its importance pales compared to the work of forgiveness designed to awaken me from a dream that, despite its dreamer's achievements, never ends happily. Kayleigh's scant weight on my arm, I called to set up an interview and then began working on transcribing my notes for another article, asking for help from my right mind to accept the idea that I do not know what anything is for, including my derailed work day, including my puppy's recurring illness; inviting the idea that I am here only to forgive, and that when I manage to do so despite my frantic busyness designed to keep me mindless my life has real meaning, the only real meaning it can have.

After a while, the vet called to say their advisor said there is no known drug-resistant strain of Giardia. Kayleigh is just small, with an undeveloped immune system. They had two new drugs to try—could I come pick them up? Oh, and I would need to bathe her daily and once again wash all items and linens she had come into contact with.

I hugged my dog and looked at my watch. I had already missed the yoga class; not that I would leave Kayleigh like this anyway. I took her outside again. Then I put her back in her crate. Another front had moved in; the sky was birthing snow. It took us a lot longer than usual to get to the vet's to pick up her additional prescriptions.

I Could See Peace

The puppy had been up several times in the night; sick again. The fan on my computer had gone ballistic and begun channeling the sound of a cement mixer. My left eye that seems to take the brunt of mysterious allergies wouldn't stop itching. Sleep deprived, worried about the dog and infuriated by the computer's drone, I couldn't seem to concentrate on the newspaper article I was trying to write. I couldn't reach the vet to discuss Kayleigh's condition either. I would have to drive over there yet again and spend another two hours waiting for them to examine her to the tune of canine torture emanating through those scary, steel doors; waiting for them to prescribe new medications administered through tiny syringes almost impossible to get her to swallow that might or might not work to cure her intestinal problems.

"I could see peace instead of this," today's *A Course in Miracle's* workbook lesson 34 suggested. I wondered what its author might be smoking.

The ego's tirade had started a couple days ago, soon after reading workbook lesson 32: "I have invented the world I see." Although the Course teaches us the world is nothing more than an outer picture of the inner condition of buried guilt in the mind, I found its wisdom hard to absorb, and quickly forgot about it as I merged into the day's many distractions and responsibilities.

My daughter had celebrated her seventeenth birthday with a sleepover the night before. She and her friends lay jumbled on the floor of our basement, limbs tangled like a three-dimensional Picasso. I tiptoed past them to the laundry room to discover my daughter had taken my half-dried load of clothes out of the dryer to accommodate her own. I switched them back. Upstairs, my husband had begun cooking bacon, sausage and waffles for the girls in the kitchen I had just cleaned up from the night before, even though it was almost 11 a.m. and they still showed no signs of stirring. On a right-minded day, I might have found it endearing. Instead, I only worried about all those Thanksgiving vegetables I needed to prep for the crowd we were having. Now I wouldn't be able to reclaim the kitchen for hours.

I took the dog into my office and decided to answer some work emails. But before I had even managed to open the first one, a slide show of grievances starring a diverse array of characters spontaneously launched itself on the screen of my brain. How could I teach *A Course in Miracles* when I couldn't seem to stop projecting? When I couldn't even remember the title of the day's workbook lesson? When all I wanted to do was let someone (and it didn't really seem to matter who) have it?

I am new to formally teaching the Course, and several of my students are completely new to studying it. I have tried to be as honest with them as possible about the Course's take on this world we think we inhabit, within which we believe we interact with others, without scaring them away. But no matter how you spin it, it is not a pretty story.

A Course in Miracles is a spiritual psychology that explains the constant conflict humans find themselves mired in, and offers a solution for resolving it at the level of the true mind, the only place in which it can be truly resolved. According to the Course, the world we think we navigate is really nothing more than an external projection of the mind's inner experience of repressed guilt over believing it separated from and in the process destroyed the one love we are and have never really left.

We naturally feel guilty over the sin we think we pulled off and fear our creator's retribution. This underlying fear motivates us to reenact on a personal level the ego's original collective projection of an entire universe of fragmented, guilt-animated forms. Blaming others for our problems momentarily relieves the mind's submerged torment, and, according to the ego, gets us off the hook with God. But quickly enough we feel guilty again and must start all over searching for a scapegoat onto whom we can cast our angry, frightened, guilty feelings. Even though none of it ever happened, the selves we think we are unconsciously believe it did and behave accordingly. I am trying to share with my students just how threatening the Course's workbook lessons, designed to expose the concealed guilt in our mind, can seem to these false selves fueled by an ego thought system intent on preventing us from ever recognizing the single source of all our misperceptions.

The workbook lessons gently invite us to begin to question the meaning, purpose and cause of our experience in this seeming world. They tell us we invented the world we see, that we could see peace instead of this parade of problems if we would learn to choose again for the part of our mind that does not take illusions seriously, the part of our mind that remembers our invulnerable unity. They encourage us to make no distinctions in our practice between inanimate objects, relationships, bodies, thoughts, traffic jams, bad hair days, sick dogs, computer glitches, wars and natural disasters because all share the same purpose of concealing the repressed "sin" of separation. They ask us to observe a world of seemingly endless, differentiated symbols and entertain the possibility that returning to our one mind might result in something other than annihilation. To entertain the possibility that returning to the scene of the "crime" of taking the "tiny mad idea" of separation from love seriously might actually empower the decision maker to whom the author of the Course speaks. That chooser in our mind once chose to believe a lie but can just as easily *choose again* for the part of our mind that remembers the truth.

I know all this and yet, going through these workbook lessons again, have once more forgotten the real cause of my seeming distress: the fear engendered by the suggestion that I could choose to see my mistaken projections through the lens of another teacher, a viewpoint that offers true comfort and release. I had felt so joyful teaching these early lessons the first few weeks and then suddenly hit a wall of resistance wherein I couldn't remember the day's lesson, let alone its point, seemingly distracted by a stream of incoming annoyances. I had fallen into the trap of trying to demonstrate how happy and loving I am, rather than recognizing and asking for help with how difficult I find it to hold on to love and happiness.

I had fallen into the trap of believing I could judge my

progress with this Course; believing that days in which I couldn't seem to stop projecting were somehow lesser than days in which I seemed to walk in an elongated holy instant. When, in truth, the workbook was working me, just as I had promised my students it would them if they sincerely applied it. Working to expose the underlying guilt we all share, the guilt we deny by projecting it outward and making it somebody else's problem. The workbook teaches us to focus on those projections, to recognize how seriously we take them and how strongly we resist changing our mind about their purpose. But we can't change our mind unless we first look outward, and we can't see truly unless we ask for help from the part of our mind that can truly see.

This is a course in bringing our darkness to the light, not bringing the light into an illusory world based on a lie. But we can't bring our darkness to the light if we don't know it's there. Jesus can't help us use our lives as a classroom and our relationships as our curriculum if we won't look with him at just how much we want to believe in a continual saga of unfair treatment at the hands of other people and situations seemingly beyond our control. We must turn to him for help in interpreting just how real we continue to make the error of separation even after years of practicing forgiveness and experiencing its mind-healing benefits. We must ask for his help again and again as we catch ourselves in the act of mindlessly projecting our fear outward. As if our lives depended on it, which, of course, the ego—intent on keeping us unaware of a life beyond the false self it invented—believes they do.

As the Light in the Dream section of Chapter 18 of the text clearly explains:

As the light comes nearer you will rush to darkness, shrinking from the truth, sometimes retreating to the lesser forms of fear, and sometimes to stark terror. But you will advance, because your goal is the advance from fear to truth. The goal you accepted is the goal of knowledge, for which you signified your willingness. Fear seems to live in darkness, and when you are afraid you have stepped back. Let us join quickly in an instant of light, and it will be enough to remind you that your goal is light.

I had fallen into the trap of believing in something external intent on disrupting my plans, my pace, my peace, my practice, the spiritual makeup I apply to disguise how deeply ticked off I truly am by this whole state of affairs we call living; this fugitive identity my false self-accusation has erected—an identity that keeps me loveless and longing, seeking but never finding, frightened and exhausted.

But I could see peace instead of this. Workbook lesson 34 does not ask us to try to prove how peaceful and spiritual we are by projecting peaceful and spiritual images on our surroundings. It asks us to search our mind for what scares us, those people and situations that trigger us. It asks us to recognize the painful emotions that surface as we do so and reassure ourselves as Jesus does that we could see peace instead of this if we will only look with him. Why? Because Jesus, the Holy Spirit, the part of our mind that holds the light of our eternal oneness, illuminates and undoes our mistaken projection, healing our tormented mind and returning us in the holy instant to the peace of the one, indivisible love we share. Nothing outside the mind ever really changes because there is nothing outside the mind. But our burden lifts, our muscles relax. Our eyes and foreheads once more serene, we recognize our brother's newly revealed innocence as our own.

Peace of mind is clearly an internal matter. It must begin with your own thoughts, and then extend outward. It is from your peace of mind that a peaceful perception of the world arises.

Notice that it says a peaceful *perception*, not a peaceful world. I could choose this.

What Does It Mean To Be Whole?

"My mind is a part of God's. I am very holy."
"My holiness envelops everything I see."
"My holiness blesses the world."
"There is nothing my holiness cannot do."
"My holiness is my salvation."

A Course in Miracles workbook lessons 35 through 39 invite us to consider the nature of holiness or *wholeness*. I have practiced these lessons before, and found them deeply comforting. Not so much this time. As I began to truly consider the idea that "my mind is part of God's," an anxious hum arose in my ears. I found it challenging to hear the lesson's words over the ego's interfering static, and even more difficult to concentrate. I felt suddenly drugged; confused and groggy. Once again I had trouble accessing the "mind" the Course addresses, the decision maker that believes it pulled off the "crime" of separating from our one, unified source from the brain that supplies me with a steady fix of three-dimensional walking, talking, interrupting, annoying, distracting, approving, rejecting, attacking, defending images upon whom to pin my peace or lack thereof.

The lesson invites us to reflect upon attributes of the individual self we think we are, the personality that interacts in an illusory world of form, the seemingly fragmented piece of the "Sonship" *A Course in Miracle's* teaches us to ultimately transcend. The lesson asks us to use various adjectives—negative and positive—to describe this fractured self, and follow each description with the declaration that we remain a part of God, healed and whole. The exercise works on a subconscious level to undo our identification with the ego thought system we allow to drive us. A thought system that has convinced us we have not only pulled off the impossible feat of dividing the indivisible; our very survival depends on compulsively projecting our "sin" outside the mind, blaming it on something or someone in a mad effort to avoid our creator's retribution. When under the influence of the ego, we behave like projecting machines, compulsively blaming the first person or situation to cross in front of our sensory apparatus for compromising our fragile peace. Sometimes, we turn the projector on our own bodies; blaming our false selves for our alleged crime and in the process experiencing physical or psychological pain.

As I wound my way through five days of the holiness lessons, my emotional and physical unrest appeared to escalate. So did the "incoming" assaults from a world I experience outside our true mind. So did my own attacks on the physical and psychological body I still think I am. Although I have been studying the Course for some time and am committed to practicing its unique form of forgiveness, I once again seemed to have trouble contacting Jesus/Holy Spirit/that part of our one mind that has never forgotten what it means to be whole and would share its knowledge if we would allow it. I asked, but nothing answered. A steady stream of outside attacks from loved ones, colleagues, and circumstances appeared to continue. The lesson's message of wholeness appeared to mock me. My wholeness *did not* envelop everything I see, I mentally complained, but my brokenness certainly did.

Seriously? I whined, by the time I got to lesson 37—"My holiness blesses the world." While I had no real trouble blessing the inanimate objects we are asked to include—I was raised Catholic, after all—I had issues with blessing my growing hit list of individuals "out there" intent on derailing my spiritual practice, despite my dedication to awakening.

Because I had been practicing the Course long enough to understand there is no one really out there, I felt caught between the proverbial rock and a hard place, paralyzed by the unconscious fear of true joining with our one inner teacher but no longer able to fully accept the ego's paranoid sob story either. And I, the decision maker, came face to face once more with our true, denied self-loathing. Useful information; I tried to tell myself. But the lessons weren't over yet. The next day, I tried to entertain the possibility that there is nothing my holiness cannot do. This lesson, in particular, entreats the decision maker to reclaim the power it believes it forfeited out of a false sense of self-preservation. It invites us to entertain the possibility that, despite our vivid dream, we remain resting in an all loving, unified, eternal, whole love that retains the only power that truly exists:

> Your holiness, then, can remove all pain, can end all sorrow, and can solve all problems. It can do so in connection with yourself and with anyone else.

Our true wholeness can eliminate all sorrow, pain, and problems because in truth, they don't exist. The lesson asks us to search our mind for any problem we see involving ourselves or anyone else and then reassure ourselves there is nothing our wholeness cannot do. Why? Because nothing ever really happened to disturb our wholeness. Despite their tantalizing and ingenious forms, our problems and all problems are actually impossible.

I did my best to follow the lesson's directions but kept forgetting to practice and found it particularly difficult to apply the idea to someone else's seeming problem as directed. I discovered I couldn't understand how others saw the situation in which we disagreed because I believed it was possible to see things differently. When, in truth, we all share the same miserable belief in the sin of separation and the same compulsive impulse to get rid of it by pinning it on someone else. I wondered if maybe that was what Jesus was inviting us to see. There is truly only one mind in need of healing because there is truly only one mind. I found that comforting, as always. I stopped fighting; stopped worrying about what the lesson meant. I merged with wholeness in the moment I gave up the struggle. My death grip on the ego relaxed and I was healed, outside time, completely cleansed of all external need. But the fear must have arisen again because I soon enough found myself observing another seeming attack, this time from someone with whom I am almost always in agreement.

"What wholeness?" the ego asked. I wanted to smack it, too.

By the time I made it to Lesson 39: "My holiness is my salvation," at the end of a long holiday weekend, I was exhausted from celebrating and entertaining and had developed an eye infection, hip, toe and elbow issues. The introverted self I think I am inwardly screamed for alone time as I cleaned up the house and fought off a cold. "If guilt is hell," the lesson began, "what is its opposite?"

"Innocence," the decision maker said.

"Heaven!" the ego shrieked. Yikes—the scene of the crime! The separation really happened; I could feel it in the pit of my stomach, despite the Course's reassuring words.

"We have already said that your holiness is the salvation of the world" I read. "What about your own salvation? You cannot give what you do not have. A savior must be saved. How else can he teach salvation?"

"My point exactly," the ego said.

I tried to ignore it but couldn't help but question how I could formally teach *A Course in Miracles* without accepting salvation for myself when all it took was a change of mind about what I really am and where my wholeness really lies? Again I asked for help; this time to stop pushing the memory of God's love away. I did what the lesson asked. I repeated the idea that my unloving thoughts about _____ and _____ and _____ were keeping me in hell but "My holiness is my salvation."

I didn't believe it; I didn't understand it; and obviously I didn't want it; but I did it anyway. And I got through my day, at least aware that there was another way of looking at these experiences that seemed so hell-bent on messing with my peace.

Fortunately, the Course meets us where we think we are on the level of form here in our dream. On the level of form, we must learn to get very good at identifying the ego in action and asking for help from our one mind that does not take the dream seriously. We need to be patient with ourselves when we stall out in the process of letting our illusions go, and recognize the fear fueling our paralysis. The Course's author, symbolic of our one awakened mind, demonstrates great patience with us. We can certainly learn to be just as tolerant and forgiving with ourselves and our process of undoing. When we fall off the forgiveness wagon, we should not berate ourselves for being mistaken and afraid. We should merely pick ourselves up and ask again for help from our right mind to know true forgiveness. That is why we are here; our only real function.

The Course tells us we need do nothing on the level of truth. Meaning the seemingly individual self I believe I am doesn't need to do anything because, in truth, the mistake of individuality never occurred, so there is nothing to do. Sometimes I get that. More often, I find it difficult to grasp in the day-to-day trenches of apparently separate interests with which I find myself grappling. Either way, I simply need to turn away from the ego's scary slide show and tune into my right mind's whole vision. I do that when I am ready. Once my fear of the unreal subsides, with help from the part of my mind that knows I have nothing to fear, I see only common interests again; the one longing to awaken we all share.

Today I awoke to Lesson 40: "I am blessed as a Son of God," feeling empty, cleansed, purged. Another toxic layer of false belief expelled; an open vessel for the one, whole, eternal light that has never stopped shining; realizing I do not know what it means to be blessed as a child of God, but am willing, and able, to learn. And in that willingness I am once again made whole.

What I Have Learned from My Dog

Over the past few months, the idea of getting a dog had blossomed in my mind. My daughter had begun to drive and would be a high school senior next year. College loomed. I also sensed my troubled relationship with our aging cat Daisy Mae drawing to a close. She had begun behaving like a person with Alzheimer's; I would catch her standing at the base of our neighbor's porch gazing upward, as if trying to figure out why someone had switched the façade on her people's house. Although I had grown terribly allergic to her dander and long since given up on her seemingly erratic (often almost feral) ways, her sudden vulnerability drew me in, along with my own need to forgive. I stood at a distance—she had always seemed more receptive to me that way—softly entreating her to come home. Semi-aware that I was not speaking literally; she seemed genuinely ready to pass on, almost transparent in the buttery autumn light. I suddenly wanted more than anything to let my grievances against this completely innocent creature go, and asked for help to do so.

When she went missing a few days later, my husband and daughter insisted she had merely hidden in someone's garage again, but I knew better. After a week had passed, we suspected she had simply crawled off somewhere to die, and hoped she had not met the more violent fate of our neighbor's cat, recently devoured by a coyote. Over the next week, denied the closure of a proper burial, we left water and food outside the garage and inside the boiler room for our ghost cat. And then, as the image of her began to recede in our psyches like a photograph developing backwards, erasing itself, devolving into white light, we found Kayleigh.

I had been researching breeds online and become quite smitten with Maltipoos (Maltese and poodle mix). Despite their embarrassing popularity among Hollywood starlets, they were extremely compact, intelligent, friendly, playful, calm, portable and hypoallergenic. As much as I love large dogs, we needed a low-maintenance animal we could lug with us on our many weekend getaways. Maltipoos seemed perfect in every respect, save the price. We could not justify dropping a couple thousand dollars on a dog. And then, browsing one night on the internet, I found an ad for a twelve-week-old Maltipoo that fit our budget, placed by a family in a nearby suburb. In the picture, she was stepping into a puddle of sunlight, staring directly into my eyes from underneath shaggy black-and-white waves. I emailed back asking if we could see her the next day. The following morning, the person who had placed the ad responded that he had someone else interested from up north, but would call if they decided to pass. I offered to drive over immediately and he agreed. The puppy we later renamed Kayleigh (which means "party" in Gaelic and aptly describes her celebratory nature) bolted into our arms and hearts and has never left.

Her prior family had bought her from a breeder a couple weeks earlier and grown concerned their two-year-old child might inadvertently hurt the tiny dog; hence the low price tag. And although we would soon drop a bundle as she battled Giardia and other intestinal infections for several weeks after joining our family, and later experienced a serious allergic reaction to her vaccinations, her robust spirit continues to belie her initially delicate physical strength. Tonight we will together attend our first puppy training class, an event we have twice postponed because of health issues. I watch her sleeping in her little bed in my office, head resting on her cloth piggy toy, and can't help but wonder who is really training whom as I reflect on all she has taught me about our true loving nature in our brief time together. Lessons such as:

1. I am loved, you are loved; he, she and it are loved: Kayleigh knows loving is her only real function. Feed her; she will lick you and wag her tail. Look at her; she will lick you and wag her tail. Come home; she will lick you and wag her tail. Talk to her; she will lick you and wag her tail. And as much as your mind on ego would like to believe you are the only one for her; she will do the same thing for anyone.

2. Love sets no conditions: I do not hold Kayleigh responsible for her mistakes in the same way I hold human beings responsible. I suppose I believe she does not share the same ego-fueled human thought system that automatically assumes ulterior motives. As *A Course in Miracles* teaches, every other individual shares my same unconscious guilty feelings over having separated from our source and my same need to get rid of those feelings by blaming them on someone else. For whatever reason, I hold Kayleigh exempt from that hidden agenda. I always give her the benefit of the doubt. When she has an accident on the floor; I speak to her firmly, clean it up and forget about it. I don't get mad at her because I see past her mistake to our essential innocence.

3. Giving and receiving are the same: I tell Kayleigh I love her. I pet her. I hold her. I talk baby-talk to her. I cuddle her; I am a veritable love machine around Kayleigh; freely doling out the love I too often withhold from others for fear of rejection or indifference. We never disagree. We never argue. She never rolls her eyes at me. She never judges. I cannot fail around this dog. In the trick mirror of her eyes, I am always welcome and adored. No matter what I do or say, she licks me and wags her tail (see number 1).

4. It never happened: Dogs know you are upset; they just don't know why. Like the Holy Spirit/right mind, they can see the illusion of the accident they just had on the rug, for example, they just know it's not really a problem in truth. They will patiently wait until your ego attack passes. Then they will lick you and wag their tail (see number 1). Then you will hold them harmless (see number 2; no pun intended).

5. The value of observing ourselves: Dogs cause grown people to refer to themselves out loud in the third person as in "Bring Mama the piggy," and "Mama loves you, yes she does; she just wishes you would do that outside instead of on the rug." This is great training for witnessing the selves we think we are from the perspective of the decision maker in our mind that chooses between the ego's perception of competing interests and the Holy Spirit's interpretation of our perfect wholeness.

6. The ego is insane: Dogs know we are rarely in our right mind. When we try to cajole them to do their business outside, as the thermometer hovers at minus twelve degrees, they dig in their heels and wait until sanity returns and we dig out the puppy training pads again. After they do what they must do, they lick us and wag their tail (see numbers 1 and 2, no pun intended).

7. Forgiveness offers everything I want. As I look past Kayleigh's seeming mistakes; as I hold her harmless in the light of our one mind, I am freed from the burden of my need to project. I know her tiny form in my life is not the one love beyond the dream but a mirror providing a generous glimpse of our unalterable, united perfection; only the eternal attraction of love for love. I don't expect her to make me happy and yet through her demonstration of boundless giving, she does. Holding her to my chest outside time in the holy instant, the one love we are returns to my mind. I notice the same loving behavior toward our dog in my husband and daughter, and find it deeply endearing. Kayleigh is teaching us to appreciate and even risk demonstrating the one love we remain and yet so often hide from each other, and from ourselves. Grateful tears well up in my eyes. She licks me and wags her tail. ☺

I Can't Get Home Without You

All week long, the individual I still believe I am has felt periodically slighted, criticized, interfered with, excluded and/or misunderstood by loved ones and those it considers close allies. (Don't even get it started on those it considers adversaries.) The nonstop, often jarring Christmas music emanating from retail store speakers doesn't help. Neither does sub-zero temperatures, icy roads, already obese "To Do" lists further bloated by holiday chores, disrupted exercise, eating and sleeping routines, and more social obligations than any introvert can reasonably be expected to handle. Like a small, overtired child pushed to the max, it doesn't want to play with you anymore. It doesn't want to share. It doesn't want to negotiate or cooperate. It doesn't want to tolerate. It wants to push all the pieces off the game board, throw itself on the floor, yell, and kick its feet. It wants someone sane, calm and loving to pick it up, take it home and fix it hot cocoa. Home, alone, away from all you nutcases.

As an *A Course in Miracles* student, I am beginning to recognize the impossibility of satisfying my true and, in truth, only desire to make it home to eternal wholeness—beyond my impossible cravings for support and solace in this world— without you. I am also beginning to recognize the mistaken belief at the root of my isolationist impulses. When "the tiny mad idea" of separation arose in the one child of God's mind and our one mind took it seriously, we believed we destroyed the infinite unity we in fact remain. Seemingly cast into a dream of opposing, fragmenting forms competing for survival, we continually search outside our apparently individual psyches for relief from the internal pain of our mistake. We find that temporary relief by projecting the repressed guilt we experience as a result of separation outward, blaming something or someone outside for our loss of peace, and then pleading with God to rescue us from the treadmill of sin, guilt, and fear we can't seem to escape on our own. But the real God, the one love we remain fused with in truth, knows nothing of our distress because the problem never happened. Enter the blessing of *A Course in Miracles'* forgiveness.

A Course in Miracles teaches us that a part of our mind transcends the ego's hallucinated universe of competing interests generated by the belief in separation and the need to protect our seemingly differentiated selves from God's retribution. The Holy Spirit/right mind holds the awareness of eternal, unified love for us. We can learn to turn away from the ego's constant rant of vulnerability and hear instead the calm, quiet voice for love that reminds us that "not one note in Heaven's song was missed." The separation never happened. We really have nothing to lose, and everything to gain, by accepting this. The Holy Spirit teaches us the benefits of acceptance when we remember to engage it. We, the decision maker that chooses between the two thought systems, "need do nothing" except *accept* atonement for ourselves by choosing for the part of our mind that believes in atonement.

All this may sound rather lofty and spiritually inflated. In truth, forgiveness, the tool we use to turn our mistaken perception over to the Holy Spirit, is dynamic and practical. It does not entreat us to refrain from blaming others for our problems. It teaches us to recognize how appealing we find differences and blame; how real incoming attacks seem when interpreted through sensory apparatus designed to prove their reality; and how unhappy our judgments make us. It asks us to watch ourselves as seeming stressors arise and inevitably escalate; to take responsibility for our mistaken illusions back to their source in the guilty ego mind, acknowledge our error and choose again for help from the part of our mind that gently smiles at the absurdity of the idea of error. When we do this, we step out of time in the "holy instant" and receive the grace of uninterrupted, eternal union. Our misperceptions and grievances burn away in the light of infinite, indivisible love; and our mind heals. Completed, beyond all external need, our perception of everyone and everything transforms and we experience only the comfort and deep release of restored unity.

I can't get home without you. That's what my loved ones and colleagues, frigid temperatures, inadequate snow removal and unfortunate holiday musical arrangements have taught me once again this week. As Chapter 15, The Two Uses of Time, makes clear:

> You will never give this holy instant to the Holy Spirit on behalf of your release while you are unwilling to give it to your brothers on behalf of theirs. For the instant of holiness is shared, and cannot be yours alone.

The ego's fear of the disintegration of the only self it knows, and punishment for the impossible crime of separation, keeps it defending this faux, finite self created to protect against the wrath of God while perpetuating its special interests. But I am not the ego. Despite my ongoing resistance, I can find a sane, loving part of my mind to lead me home. I need but focus on my curriculum. I need but notice my mistaken interpretations of the problems and perpetrators I have created to keep me from returning to the source of the only real problem in the one mind. I need but remember I want to go home, and so does every single other nutcase "out there." We all share the same miserable, repressed belief in guilt, the same fear of punishment, and the same compulsion to blame others. And we all share the deep longing to return to the boundless comfort of our true nature. The loving hand that guides us home is always patiently extended at the border of our mistaken illusions. I find it again, along with our unwavering innocence, by extending my hand once more to you regardless of what the ego would have me believe you have done.

Christmas as the End of Sacrifice

I awoke this morning aching with an all-too-familiar melancholy that often cripples me in December; sandwiched in between all the music and shopping, happy talk and sugar and striving to perfect and please; despite a thermometer yielding welcome mild temperatures following a nearly two-week deep freeze; despite a sun high in a sky blue enough to evoke Italian Renaissance paintings spilling pinkish light and casting deep, satisfying shadows; despite a comforting silence as I allowed the dog who has not exactly gotten the hang of this walking on a leash thing to root away in the dry grass like a truffle-sniffing pig; despite the perfect stillness that always seems to follow a day of high winds here in this dualistic world of competing interests; despite squirrels darting hopefully about, hoarding for the future, I could feel winter's bleakness in my bones today, the heaviness of the human condition, the suffering my choice for specialness continues to bring when I resist changing my mind.

And yet I am also thinking about light: the literal variety my neighbors have once again beat us to festooning their houses with, the tradition of lighting up the darkness at Christmas and Hanukah, and the hope of early civilizations enticing the sun to return to warm their fields. And the symbol of light *A Course in Miracles* uses to remind us of the one, abstract, whole, loving presence that still shines within our seemingly split mind. Despite our attraction to the darkness of continuing to exclude as we perceive ourselves excluded, to attack as we perceive ourselves attacked. Despite the ego's appealing argument that we must curry favor to get our needs met here in this world through what the Course calls "sacrifice;" giving to get in our special relationships; bargaining with those people, objects, and substances we continue to substitute for the real love we believe we catastrophically destroyed.

I am thinking about the idea of bringing the darkness of guilt that hides in my mind over that mistaken belief to the light of our right mind's truth once and for always, releasing the weight of this seasonal sadness as the year winds down, once more failing to deliver the perfect happiness my mind on ego continues to seek where it can never be found. I am entertaining the possibility of truly, madly, deeply surrendering the idea that I can ever find happiness in this world, resigning for good as my own teacher, and fully embracing the only teacher that can truly guide me home, and the only teaching I truly want to learn. What would happen if I embraced the light here, now, and forever? Susan would disappear. And there's the rub. Because a part of me still fears the light, craves darkness in which to hide and simultaneously covets my unique identity; however unstable and no matter the cost.

How do I find the light when I still fear it? By beginning to recognize how much my mistaken belief in the original idea of separation has cost me; by learning to associate all my judgments of others, all my striving to complete myself with something or someone outside me with that original choice; and by learning through experience that when I bring the darkness of my mistaken illusions to the light in my mind that continues to eternally shine, I am once more made whole, restored to and completed in the love I am. I do this from moment to moment with help from the part of my mind that remembers my perfect wholeness in what the Course calls the "holy instant:" that abstract place outside time where the guilt I have tried to deny by casting it on you dissolves in the united, eternal, indivisible love we share.

I awoke this morning feeling unloved and unloving, separate and sad, following a weekend in which I experienced the most extraordinary healing. My family and I picked out our Christmas tree, strung it with lights, decorated it and went on to decorate the entire house without a single sharp word or slamming door. I did not once mutter as I dusted off the singing Christmas bass or talking Santa Claus head my husband continues to find hilarious. No one got upset when the lights didn't work and my husband disappeared into the labyrinth of Home Depot, the place our daughter once accused him of secretly holding a second job because he spent so much time there. She did not roll her eyes once as I obsessively rearranged the figures in our crèche. It didn't bother me at all when she failed to hang the ornaments to swing freely; I did not even feel compelled to re-hang them.

We worked together methodically amid the clutter, now and then joining in with the carols she picked out, sipping Cokes and Vitamin Waters. At one point, standing beside my daughter and reaching to hang the Eiffel Tower ornament my friend Beth had given me years earlier, the unified peace we all share washed over me and I could feel my child's arm reaching in tandem as my own, our seeming separate bodies irrelevant in the truth of our oneness. As the hours passed, our perfect Christmas expectation-riddled script at last abandoned, the darkness set in outside and our tree sparkled with new LED lights. Our puppy asleep on the velveteen tree skirt, we treated ourselves to sushi takeout.

And yet, I awoke this morning siding with the ego again, mentally blaming others for yet another winter of my discontent, the slide show of the year's unfulfilled wishes and broken promises flashing in my head; having once more mistaken the classroom of this world for a playground; having forgotten that playing may satisfy children for a while, but only learning the one lesson of forgiving the incredible belief that anyone or thing outside my mind can jeopardize my essential happiness delivers the mature and lasting love I crave.

Fortunately, I have experienced the ego's backlash before and am learning not to take it seriously. After all, I made it all up. I am learning that I want to hold you harmless; I want to stop buying, wrapping, rushing, baking and striving to win back the love I think I have forsaken, and love to accuse of forsaking me. When I have chosen our right mind as my teacher I want to be whole and healed. I want to see things differently because it makes me feel better. I am learning that anything other than perfect peace of mind reflects that original, albeit unconscious, choice I made to push love away; but I want love back. I really have nothing to lose in choosing again for the only love that actually exists, and everything to gain. Nothing outside my mind can make me feel better or compromise the peace I am. The prison door remains open. When I choose your release, I am finally free. This Christmas, rereading Christmas as the End of Sacrifice in Chapter 15, I am learning I truly *want* to:

> ...give the Holy Spirit everything that would hurt you. Let yourself be healed completely that you may join with Him in healing, and let us celebrate our release together by releasing everyone with us...Make this year different by making it all the same. And let all your relationships be made holy for you. This is our will. Amen.

What Does It Mean To Be Happy?

I have just returned from a family ski vacation in Crested Butte, the quintessential Colorado ski town that, despite its recent growing pains, still evokes a place that time forgot. News is scare, cell phones and DSL signals unreliable, restaurant and retail service orchestrated to the beat of a different drummer. The gingerbread-style storefronts on Elk Avenue hunch beneath the weight of the season's perennial snowfall much as they did a century ago. School buses painted with psychedelic scenes by local artists still blast Woodstock-era ballads while snaking their way up to the ski mountain carrying a curious cargo of Texans, Southerners, local families, Gunnison ranchers, and single dudes and dudettes intent on cobbling together an alternative, sustainable lifestyle.

I initiated the tradition of spending the week after Christmas here several years ago hoping to capture a saner way to ring in my least favorite holiday in a setting more conducive to intro-spection and renewal, surrounded by those I love. In the years that followed, I have come to better comprehend the true nature of sanity and the folly of believing it has anything to do with time, venue, company or an introvert craving contemplation. I am learning through studying and practicing *A Course in Miracles* that, despite appearances, life is merely a classroom for the lessons of awakening from this dream of separate interests, its relationships and circumstances the curriculum I use to undo the idea that I have any other function than forgiving my belief that anyone or thing seemingly outside our one mind can in any way affect my true wellbeing.

Last year, for example, I broke my hip on New Year's Day walking too fast on ice in the parking lot of the local grocery store: an ordeal I later wrote about that forced me to consider the motivation behind my compulsive urgency as well as my need (even on the level of form) to separate myself from those I love. This year, my lessons seem more subtle, although the Course makes no such worldly distinctions among illusions. I have been teaching a class on the Course's workbook and over the week considered workbook lesson 66: "My happiness and my function are one." The lesson contrasts the world's view of happiness, the result of getting what we think we want, with the Course's version, the result of recognizing we have no idea what would make us happy and turning to a teacher that does know and can teach us.

Over the week, as I found myself once again reviewing the year and attempting to apply the lessons, I again and again caught myself listening to the ego's all-too convincing arguments: I had not met this or that writing goal; I still judged others, withheld love, and experienced periodic turmoil in my closest relationships; I still craved external approval that seemed in short supply. I had exhausted myself preparing for Christmas and once more felt like I had somehow missed the whole thing. I was fighting my annual sinus infection and couldn't even ski as well as I had before the fracture. My hip throbbed and I still slept poorly. What kind of Course student was I?

The ego does constant battle with the Holy Spirit on the fundamental question of what your function is. So does it do constant battle with the Holy Spirit about what your happiness is. It is not a two-way battle. The ego attacks and the Holy Spirit does not respond. He knows what your function is. He knows that it is your happiness.

The Holy Spirit, that lofty name for the memory of our true wholeness that followed us into this dream of duality, does not respond to illusions, but simply waits for us to look with it and choose again. The Course tells us over and over that we have only one function—forgiveness or choosing again for the Holy Spirit's vision—and that learning to accept our function will bring us the only enduring happiness possible: happiness that arises from the only real source of happiness, the one indivisible love we believe we destroyed but have actually never left; that one, stable love in which we continue to rest, dreaming of exile.

Forgiveness, *A Course in Miracles* style, has nothing to do with our pleasure or lack of it in this world. It doesn't indulge illusory, romantic, chick flick endings. Instead, it asks us to consider what happens after the couple sails into the sunset; how invested we are in denying our essential unhappiness that stems from the unconscious belief that we separated from love; how much we enjoy blaming our lack of happiness on someone else. What happens when our significant other fails to meet our needs? When a child we have nurtured hits puberty and seems to turn against us? When the worldly recognition we believe we earned fails to materialize? When an employer for whom we have "selflessly" slaved for years lays us off? What happens on the inside when the characters and circumstances in the projected-outside-the-mind dream fail us, as they inevitably do? We go ballistic, that's what; compulsively projecting our anger on those we hold responsible for our suffering, acting out the ego's script that keeps us from ever returning to the decision maker in the one mind that can choose a different teacher.

Forgiveness is the process that restores our mind to the eternally happy state of wholeness. If we choose not to forgive, we are choosing unhappiness. The only real choice is for the ego or the Holy Spirit, no matter how ingenious and tantalizing, upsetting and convincing the dream's specifics appear to the body's senses. Heaven or hell? Dream or awakening? Classroom or playground in which someone always gets hurt and someone always feels guilty and fearful of punishment? I am finally learning how much I really don't want to be happy; how much I prefer chasing happiness guaranteed to fail me; how the pursuit maintains the ego's secret goal of specialness while keeping me forging back into the world for yet another fix of fleeting pleasure, seeking for happiness where it can never be found in a future that doesn't exist.

The section of the Course's text called The Happy Dream in Chapter 18 offers us a very clear process for reclaiming the happiness we blame others for jeopardizing. It invites us to join our mind with the Holy Spirit in the "holy instant:" that place outside time in which the mistaken belief of separation and separate interests is healed, leaving only the loving happiness we share. It offers us a forgiveness prayer for whoever is "saner at the time" to apply to any seemingly "out there" relationship/problem, allowing the Holy Spirit to heal our mind about the "problem" of separate interests as we join with it in the holy instant of our release.

If I have chosen the Course to lead me home, looked honestly, and recognized that all the world's goals have ultimately failed me, I am the one that must catch myself once more siding with the ego's insanity. I must remember that it only takes one mind to heal the illusion that there could possibly be more than one mind in need of healing. With this choice, I experience gratitude for the restored wholeness my relationships offer me when I change my mind about their purpose—from proving separation and opposition to proving eternal unity and common interests. I accept the holy instant of changed perception for myself as I remember I still love this seemingly challenging "other" because there is ultimately no other and infinitely only one inclusive love. With this recognition, I begin to forgive myself for pushing love away, and develop compassion for everyone else experiencing the same miserable ego thought system that keeps them seeking for love and happiness in all the wrong places.

And so I will once more try to accept and allow my only real function, forgiveness, as I begin this New Year, turning the undoing of my false belief in separate interests over to a teacher that remembers what I really want; trying to remember that the ego's forever unfulfilled promises mean nothing, and that choosing that understanding brings me a little closer to awakening to real happiness with you.

Only God's Plan for Salvation Will Work

The dog was scheduled for spaying Friday morning. I dropped her off between 7 and 7:30 as instructed. It had taken about twenty minutes to defrost the car and scrape the latticework of ice that had enveloped the windshields overnight courtesy of the latest arctic blast. Kayleigh whimpered and shivered in my jacket as we got out of the car in the hospital parking lot. I once again pushed away a nagging dread that had plagued me all night as I waded in and out of sleep, the puppy mimicking my positions as she does when I allow her to sleep beside me. I had no problem with getting her spayed but something just didn't feel right about this.

We waited in the short line with other groggy dog owners before I placed her on the scale. My anxiety increased as I noticed she had actually dropped a couple of ounces over the holidays in her frantic efforts to please a houseful of people, weighing in at only 3.2 pounds. As I filled out multiple forms, I realized they had whisked my little lightweight away without my even noticing, without even allowing me to hug her goodbye. Something just didn't feel right about this.

I returned to my home office to read and practice that day's workbook lesson 71: "Only God's plan for salvation will work," and couldn't help but marvel anew at the author's uncanny ability to illuminate the ego's plan for our salvation/happiness in passages such as:

> According to this insane plan, any perceived source of salvation is acceptable provided that it will not work. This ensures that the fruitless search will continue, for the illusion persists that, although this hope has always failed, there is still grounds for hope in other places and in other things. Another person will yet serve better; another situation will yet offer success.

Poised at the launch of the New Year, I had been sorely tempted over the past week to once more invest in the ego's insane agenda for external happiness that cannot last, that must—like the bodies and forms it appears to support—wither and die. This got me thinking about the special relationship I had immediately forged with my puppy. I had come close to losing her before and wasn't sure I could bear it, despite the Course's comforting words about the fallacy of individuality and the eternal comfort of our true nature. I pictured her tiny form sedated on the vast, cold, steel operating table like a speck of gravel on an airport runway. I pulled my sweater in around me as I returned to the lesson, seeking outside myself once again for peace, as if the Course itself were a panacea for my worry, rather than the choice of different inner teacher it offered.

God's plan for salvation will work, and other plans will not.

Do not allow yourself to become depressed or angry at the second part; it is inherent in the first.

Over winter break vacation, I had taken a morning off from skiing with my family and friends to go snowshoeing, Kayleigh on my back in the new dog backpack my friend Darla had given me for Christmas. It was snowing, the light flat. I headed up the hill from the Nordic Center. As I climbed the undulating trails overlooking the town of Crested Butte, a cloud of snow suddenly enveloped the steepled Victorian rooftops and the butte itself. In near zero visibility, I trundled on a ways before stopping to savor the stillness, completely disoriented, completely OK with absolute nothingness. Steeped in an elongated moment in which I lost track of my body and my dog's, the bondage of our seeming place in time and space, and the brutal myth of individuality. Although apparently lost, I felt found, swaddled in a deep sense of comfort and release, my usual fears of the elements and predators at bay. After a while, an anemic sun beamed through the milky sky and my bearings returned. I hiked for another hour or so before returning to our rental.

Now I sat in my office contemplating God's plan for salvation: forgiving the illusion of this body, that body, and all bodies seemingly dueling for fleeting survival, and, in so doing, restoring the eternal nothingness of the whole, one, inalterable love we are, versus the ego's perennial "To Do" list designed to keep us firmly rooted in a cloudy, frantic, frightening dream. The lesson goes on to invite us to ask God to specifically reveal his plan for our salvation by asking what he would have us do, where he would have us go, what he would have us say and to whom? When I first read these words, I had, like most students, taken them literally, believing that God knew about my unique fantasies and the "me" that fantasized. But I continued to practice forgiveness, turning my projections over to the part of our one mind that remembers there is nothing to do, nowhere to go, and nothing to say because there is (ultimately) no self to say it and no "other" to say it to. This allowed a deeper experience of healing to permeate my mind: a healing that now helped me provide right-minded answers to these questions our inner teacher would have me pose to the God the ego would like us to believe we have forsaken:

"What would You have me do?"
Forgive.
"Where would You have me go?"
To the Holy (Whole) Spirit in my mind.
"What would You have me say, and to whom?"

Holy Spirit, please help me to see/experience everything in this dream of seeming "specialness" with your awareness.

My concern for my puppy's welfare, my belief that I could lose the one love we share that she so gracefully reflects back to the me, abated as I allowed my right mind to answer. A couple of hours later, the doctor called to explain that while trying to place the breathing tube into Kayleigh's trachea before putting her under anesthesia she had begun coughing and they had not been able to fit the tube in properly. She was OK, but still loopy from sedation and very stressed out. It was too dangerous to proceed; they would have to postpone the spaying. I put the big, blue book away and rescheduled a couple of meetings. Then I went back out into the cold to pick up my dog.

The Light Has Come

Last weekend I saw the movie *A Single Man*, the story of a gay college English professor named George living in Southern California circa 1962 and grieving the recent accidental death of his long-time, live-in lover Jim. Based on the novel by Christopher Isherwood, the plot follows actor Colin Firth through a single day at the end of which he intends to put an end to his unrelenting grief by committing suicide. With his usual endearing restraint, Firth demonstrates the ego thought system's suffering over the secret, albeit universal, sense of isolation we all share caused by the mistaken belief that we have separated from our one source and in so doing destroyed it.

The movie's title speaks to the deep loneliness we all carry as a result of that forgotten choice, if we are truly honest with ourselves. As a Brit living in the U.S. and a gay man living in a pre-sexual-liberation era, Firth experiences himself so completely "outside" that the loss of his only real love leaves him little reason to continue. His one friend, Charley, a delightful British lush played by Julianne Moore, feels equally victimized by life's circumstances and thereby incapable of providing any lasting support or solace.

The story of George's relationship with his lover (actor Mathew Goode) evolves through flashback; in an early scene George answers the phone to hear about the car accident that killed Jim from a distant relative who explains that the family has excluded George from the funeral. The film captures the quiet, committed nature of the couple's special, if forbidden, love: a love George credits with whatever happiness he has experienced in this world; the memory of which keeps him firmly rooted in the past and largely incapable of interacting in the present.

As he traverses this final ordinary day made extraordinary by his hidden agenda, we observe him again and again literally merging with the light in elongated moments (what the Course calls holy or whole instants) wherein he truly connects with others in spite of himself: a little neighbor girl, an admiring student who may or may not have more on his mind than ideas, a chance, chaste encounter with a male prostitute. In these and other scenes the movie's stark—bordering-on-film-noir—palette, suddenly warms and softens. Buttery color returns to Firth's face along with a smile as he momentarily chooses to look past his dire interpretation of his story and reconnect with the true vision of right-minded unity that transcends his tragic individuality.

I am thinking about the movie *A Single Man* as I contemplate *A Course in Miracles* workbook lesson 75: "The light has come," which begins so cheerfully:

The Light has come. You are healed and you can heal. The light has come. You are saved and you can save.

The lesson describes the "real world," the Course's description of the world we will experience once we have forgiven all our mistaken perceptions of unfair treatment, competing interests, and irreconcilable differences. "Today we celebrate the happy ending to your long dream of disaster," it reassures us; even though most Course students aren't exactly ready to start cracking open the champagne any time soon. For most of us, the ending—that promised awakening from the illusory nightmare of exile—can appear far off even as we practice turning our dark perceptions over to the light of the Holy Spirit in our one mind where they burn away. Only to be replaced by another illusory attack seemingly launched from "out there" about which we must once more change our mind. That's because, although we could in theory instantly awaken, in practice we are far too fearful of retribution for the crime we believe we pulled off and far too attracted to the idea of specialness and the mad possibility that the future will somehow offer something better than the past.

For most of us, the undoing of the ego thought system promised in *A Course in Miracles* through forgiveness is a process that appears to transpire over time even though on the level of truth the mistaken idea of separation from our source was instantly corrected. It meets us where we think we are, in the fragmented condition we think we are in. It teaches us to begin to associate the loss of peace we enjoy blaming on someone or thing external with an internal problem, the cause of all subsequent problems, that initial belief in the concept of duality. It teaches us first to identity the decision maker in our mind that made that initial choice and can choose again to turn our mistaken belief over to the part of our mind that can heal it. When we do this we feel better, which motivates us to choose more and more for peace whenever we find ourselves in seeming pain. Practicing forgiveness, the guilt in our seemingly split mind over the idea of separation gradually heals until we have forgiven everything outside we have tried to use to hurt ourselves. The bogus individuality to which the ego clings dissolves in the light of our true, loving, eternal grandeur.

We reclaim that grandeur by seeing our relationships differently, by reaching out to others in the holy instant in which we choose true vision and experience the transcendence of inner darkness to light. We find our grandeur as we symbolically extend a hand in our suffering to those we once held responsible and find ourselves instead grasping our own forever unified innocence.

What I love about this movie with Colin Firth (on whom I have always had a bit of a crush along with almost every other female of my generation) is the brutal emotional honesty he expresses through the character of George: a man who has come to the end of the dream to witness with an unwavering gaze the final result of the ego thought system; a man who has reached a point we all must eventually reach (to be motivated to awaken) wherein we recognize the true hopelessness of finding anything but fleeting happiness in this world. And then he goes bravely on to recognize that true connection with the only relationship that can endure and offer lasting love begins with turning our darkened images of others over to the memory of the light that continues to shine in our one mind.

Without giving too much of the ending away, suffice it to say that George pulls something like this off, at least through enough transformative holy instants to ultimately change his mind about his plans and plight, and his harrowing sense of isolation; at least enough to change his mind about his interpretation of what seems to be happening to him, the Course's radical definition of a miracle.

Love Makes No Comparisons

Normally things seem to slow down after the holidays and I savor burrowing bear-like into my den. I sleep in (for me that amounts to first light around 7 a.m.), read, putter around the house, watch movies, and dig out the crock pot to whip up the kind of comfort fare so compatible with truncated days and elongated, chilly nights. The phone doesn't ring as much as usual, social engagements dwindle, and emails and work projects grind to a halt, allowing the introvert in me to languish content, seemingly free of the usual external pressures. Not this January.

This January has been downright insane, or so the ego frequently insists in its 24/7 fireside chats. Incoming phone calls and emails bring constant new demands and my social calendar appears to have spiraled out of control without my participation. I have done a lot of mental whining about this and yesterday finally succumbed to that attacking voice in my head, awakening to dizziness, nausea, and a weak cough on a Monday morning when I had planned to get so much done. Finally carving out the down time I thought I needed by demonstrating through my apparently diseased body that I just couldn't take it anymore.

Unable to think straight or interact, I turned off the computer and cancelled a lunch I'd been looking forward to with a dear friend I don't see often enough. I took my rightful place on the couch with a bowl of chicken noodle soup, a pot of ginger tea, and my little lap dog to indulge my suffering with an episode of *Desperate Housewives*, that long-running TV satire about the ego's triumphs and tribulations lived out through special relationships run amuck on a superficially idyllic Wisteria Lane.

In this episode, Susan and Gabby become obsessed with their children's ratings at the snazzy private elementary school where Susan teaches art and her son attends classes with Gabby's daughter. Hoping to prevent parents from engaging in the kind of competitive behavior over their kids' status parents all too often do, the school has named the math and reading groups after animals and refrains from disclosing the hierarchy of what it means to be a giraffe, a leopard, or a chipmunk, for example. New to the school, Gabby tries to wrestle the information out of Susan, who believes she can discern where students fit academically by the level of their artistic ability in her class. She implies that Gabby's daughter is in the lowest group, launching Gabby into a full-blown ego attack in which she sets out to break the code by photographing her daughter and her friends' homework assignments and comparing the level of complexity.

We laugh at such ridiculous antics because, although most of us wouldn't go quite that far to prove our children's superiority (and through association our own), most of us have engaged in just such petty fantasies in our heads. While we may try to deny and conceal the form of our compulsion to compare, the content rings true if we are honest with ourselves. All comedy springs from this place of poking fun at the human condition: the condition in which we believe we find ourselves marooned here on a planet of opposites and opposition, fighting to distinguish ourselves from the pack, to "save" ourselves from the consequences of our own repressed guilty impulses at someone else's expense.

A Course in Miracles speaks to us on the level of truth—the unified wholeness in which we continue to rest dreaming of exile and experimenting with hallucinated individuality—when it tells us that "love makes no comparisons." But in this illusory world we take so seriously, on the level of form in which we believe we operate acting as mindless robots of the ego thought system, we compare ourselves constantly. Why? Because it proves the ego's belief that something different exists to compare. Differences mean we operate separately in different bodies with different characteristics and talents, limitations and agendas, leading different lives of desperation, with different goals and story arcs of inclusion and exclusion. As Chapter 24's The Treachery of Specialness observes:

> Comparison must be an ego device, for love makes none. Specialness always makes comparisons. It is established by a lack seen in another and maintained by searching for, and keeping clear in sight, all lacks it can perceive. This does it seek, and this it looks upon.

No wonder these housewives are desperate! We're all desperate when we listen to the ego; desperate to seek and find a different solution to the perceived problem of specialness, a different outcome to the painful sense of lack and guilt we carry over the denied "sin" of separation; desperate to prove a hierarchy of illusions reflective of the only problem that exists (our belief that we have separated from the one love we are and in truth remain); desperate to project the nagging lack of love we feel as a result and constantly deny on someone else. We do it through comparison.

> And always whom it thus diminishes would be your savior, had you not chosen to make of him a tiny measure of your specialness instead. Against the littleness you see in him you stand as tall and stately, clean and honest, pure and unsullied, by comparison with what you see. Nor do you understand it is yourself that you diminish thus.

I have spent most of my life comparing myself to others favorably and unfavorably. Whether I seek to enlarge my false self in the trick mirror of another's eyes or diminish my false self by ticking off its meager accomplishments and talents compared to those of other seemingly greater false selves this time around, the intent and result are the same. Either way, I am coveting the "littleness" of individuality I have chosen over the grandeur of my true, one, boundlessly loving and creative nature: an *abstract* nature that has nothing to do with the me I think compares.

Whether this false me seeks to reinforce my specialness with my child's report card, the relative perfection or difficulty of my marriage, worldly successes, acquisitions, or failures; or to pinpoint exactly how far I have come in understanding *A Course in Miracles* in relationship to others, I am choosing fleeting pleasure or unique suffering over eternal happiness beyond my current understanding. That understanding returns to my mind little by little through the holy (whole) instant in which I turn away from the ego's comparisons and awaken to the (whole) Spirit's memory of a loving, non-dualistic self in which comparisons are impossible because there is no one with whom to compare. When I choose to forgive, I release all my beliefs about this false self and all those other false selves I think I see up there on the screen of my brain, literally projected by my wrong mind. I am healed of my need to identify my child's reading group and can once more smile gently with our inner teacher at a comic fiction that—thank God—could never really be.

I Don't Want To Be Responsible Anymore!

The big house in the dream seems simultaneously familiar and unfamiliar, although I know I used to live here and am apparently doing so again for unknown reasons. Hosting a surprise party for someone, although I seem to have forgotten who, a dirty little secret I'm afraid to share. I thought others were bringing the food and drinks but apparently I am in charge. The mother of one of my daughter's friends arrives along with a few other women I supposedly know but can't seem to place. I apologize and rush out to purchase appetizers and wine, attempting to reach various people (including my husband and daughter) to help me, without success.

Caught in traffic on my way to Whole Foods, I attempt a shortcut through the neighborhoods and become hopelessly lost. I pass a yard and notice an old acquaintance I have not seen in years sitting on a lawn chair conversing with neighbors outside a small refurbished Victorian home, and suddenly identify her as the guest of honor at this party I am apparently throwing. I'm not even sure I invited her! In a complete panic, I inexplicably make a U-turn and end up in a part of town I have never encountered before.

I find an Italian deli and try to order appetizers but the proprietors appear to be moving in slow motion. I realize I won't have time to make it to the wine store and decide to buy wine from the Italians but everything is ridiculously overpriced and I can't get anyone to help me with a row of unmarked bottles. My cell keeps ringing but I don't answer it, convinced people are arriving at this other house—guests I allegedly invited—only to find no host, no guest of honor, and no food or drink. I am told it was all my idea, but an idea I don't even remember having! The Italians just stare, dragging themselves around without speaking in their heavy, dark clothes in overexposed light, as if in a Bergman film. Overcome with dizziness, I feel I might perish on the spot from guilt.

"I don't want to be responsible anymore!" I awaken, screaming in my head.

All week long, I have been secretly shouting this mantra. *I don't want to be responsible anymore!* Not for setting up this interview, writing this article, shopping for and cooking another dinner for a family that never sits down to eat, filling out and copying my daughter's athletic and community service trip forms. Not for taking the dog to the vet again, straightening up other people's ubiquitous messes, making travel arrangements and setting up college tours for Spring break. I want *you* to be responsible for a change. Is that too much to ask?

But as I lay awake still shuddering with dread completely out of proportion to the circumstances of the dream, reviewing the ego's litany of suffering at the hands of all those I felt unfairly responsible for, I truly understood the *real* responsibility I had been attempting to duck all my life. Responsibility for the original "sin" of separating from our source, an impossible, unconscious crime the Course tells us we try to atone for by blaming others; in this case, by playing "the responsible one" in my relationships while mentally whining: "Why can't *you* be responsible for a change?"

I am desperately trying to prove to God through sacrifice that I could not have pulled this off; look how responsible (in a good way) I am and have always been. These other shiftless ones must have done it! And yet, in my heart of hearts, I knew I was the real guilty one. I believed I had run away from my father's home and murdered him on the way out the door just like the Course says: a crime no amount of hand-washing or doing for others can ever fully expunge from my record.

Of course I was listening to the ego again, once more inviting the wrong part of our one mind to twist the Course's metaphysics to make the error of my belief in the idea of separation real, thereby strengthening my special story of living as a fugitive from love here in this impossible dream of opposing interests. Intent on continuing to frighten me into its fold of specialness, the ego had omitted the only *true* message in *A Course in Miracle's* creation myth: the separation from love never happened. Or, to put it poetically as the Course often does: "Not one note in heaven's song was missed."

Oddly enough, I had been working with *A Course in Miracles* workbook lesson 93: "Light and joy and peace abide in me." Sounds promising, doesn't it? And yet it begins like this:

You think you are the home of evil, darkness and sin. You

think if anyone could see the truth about you he would be repelled, recoiling from you as if from a poisonous snake. You think if what is true about you were revealed to you, you would be struck with horror so intense that you would rush to death by your own hand, living on after seeing this being impossible.

Beware these cheerful lesson titles that almost always go on to smack you upside the head with the flip side of our true, indivisible, eternally peaceful nature: the side the ego has convinced us will strike us dead should we ignore its advice and dare to look. Although these lessons often convey the truth about ourselves in our pre-dream state, they also attempt to meet us in the hell of the condition in which we seem to find ourselves dreaming our fugitive dreams of exile from love; following the ego's plan for salvation by denying responsibility for having separated from our eternal wholeness; locking our guilt away in the recesses of our unconscious only to have it come spewing forth into our waking and sleeping dreams; compelling us to compulsively cast it outside ourselves again by seeing it in someone else.

But I am learning I am not responsible for separating from and thereby destroying God and neither are you. There's no need to commit hara-kiri over a crime that never happened. I am learning I am not the ego; I am the decision maker that chose to believe in and feel responsible for the tiny mad idea of separation and the consequences the ego convinced me loom. I am the decision maker that chose to feel responsible for something that never occurred, but can learn, as I practice the workbook lessons and apply the Course's principles in my daily life, to choose a different teacher with a different interpretation of ultimately non-existent events.

The self you made is not the Son of God. Therefore, this self does not exist at all. And anything it seems to do and think means nothing. It is neither bad nor good. It is unreal, and nothing more than that.

When I consciously choose to take responsibility for my projected guilt onto others back to the source of the original mistaken idea in our one mind, the Holy (Whole) Spirit heals my perception of this false, guilty self and the dualistic idea of responsibility and I experience our oneness. I need but learn to truly look with the part of my one mind that can truly see. By accepting my only real function of forgiveness, responsibility for the root cause of suffering is removed from others, accepted in myself, and then instantly released as we join our mind with the Holy Spirit and gently smile at an ultimately incomprehensible, impossible dream.

Wag More, Bark Less

My little dog Kayleigh spends a lot of time peering out our side glass door into the frozen garden as dusk descends, now and then issuing a determined woof, guarding us from illusory predators. As often as not, she spies my shadow moving behind her in the kitchen or perhaps her own, mistakes it for an encroaching enemy, and, like any faithful guard dog, springs into alert mode. Occasionally, she graces us with a single, ferocious bark, before hopping backwards with a little snort like the Cowardly Lion in the *Wizard of Oz*. Reacting and overreacting to her mistaken interpretations—my morphing shadow and her own—the dark side of maltipoos is clearly exposed.

I can't help but relate. I was the kind of kid that saw a continuous parade of monsters and witches writhing on the windows and walls of my bedroom. There were beings out to get us in this world; I knew it even as a toddler: beings in the basement, beings in the attic, beings in the closet and under the bed that did not have our best interests at heart. The Commies could launch nuclear missiles at any moment from the other side of the world that could wipe us out in a single, gigantic mushroom blast. A person could have a heart attack like the mother of one of our friends across the street or an explosion in their brain like my cousin's wife and drop dead. I counted catastrophes instead of sheep lying in bed as a child. And yet, there was something addictive even back then about it all, a thrill I preferred not to examine too closely, endlessly distracted by defending against all these horrifically entertaining shadows.

My brother Michael and I would burrow under the covers in my bed on rainy mornings listening over and over again to the score from Prokofiev's *Peter & the Wolf*. Our mother would put the record on the turntable, then go about her housewifely business. The vivid music and tale of a daring, disobedient boy's near-death encounter with a wolf seriously creeped us out. We would scream at the top of our lungs as Peter and his animal friends acted out their parts in a story of Communist propaganda completely lost on us. I credit the score for my early fascination with all things Russian (including, I suppose, that ever likely to detonate in my backyard bomb) and my later decision to take up the clarinet in elementary school in honor of my favorite character Ivan the cat.

But I digress once again, as the ego would have me do. The point is I am coming to the end of a year in which I committed to remember to look at my errors in perception with my right mind and report in writing at least weekly on the results. Not in an attempt to stare the many forms the one error seems to take down or growl the ego's fantasies into submission but to watch them disappear in the light of true vision when I choose to open the garden door that appears to keep love away and step into the light, allowing a smile to return to my mind.

We have been applying the workbook's "happiness lessons" (workbook lessons 101-103) in the class I am teaching on forgiveness in which our teacher, that symbol of the awakened

222

mind we all share, entreats us to consider our true will and nature versus our mind on ego. "God's Will for me is perfect happiness," he tells us. "I share God's Will for happiness for me" and "God, being Love, is also happiness." He tells us we do not want to suffer, that joy is our inheritance. But Jesus also tells us we deny this truth, intent on making the "sin" of separation from our unified, loving source real by projecting the guilt it engenders in our unconscious mind onto someone else, compulsively blaming the shadow "out there" for our unhappiness in an effort to cajole God into buying our relative innocence. We're addicted to looking with the ego at seemingly infinite manifestations of that same murderous story, defending and attacking our own shadow in endless guises. So frantically distracted by battling our own image that we forget we can summon the other teacher in our one mind and learn to smile at these theatrics.

Why do we crave looking with the body's eyes despite the pain it brings? Why are we so afraid to look with our right mind even though it offers real happiness over surreal terror? Because if God equals the only real love there is and we sinned against him, we must keep love away or face certain retaliation. And so we defend against love, terrified to look beyond the murky, murderous figures competing for survival in the mirror.

Confronted with the peace and joy of our true nature, these lessons had once more plunged me (the decision maker that once chose for the ego's impossible dream of exile from love and clings to its mistaken fugitive identity) into a fearful abyss. This is not a nice world. When I look with Susan's eyes I am not a happy camper; battling myriad confounding problems casting their shadows on the glass of my brain. Forgetting I am really gazing into a trick mirror at the illusory face of my own false self, a fearful image generated by a stray thought that could never be.

I had been taking it all, including this Course, seriously again; looking with my wrong mind, judging what I saw, and confusing adrenaline and the promise of specialness with the serene, eternal happiness I really wanted. Once again my little dog had mirrored my wrong mind back to me, allowing me to recognize my error and choose again to look with a teacher that can truly see.

It has been a year since I committed to catching myself looking with the ego and choosing instead to look with the Holy (Whole) Spirit in our *one* mind. I am still afraid, but I am at least learning that developing the habit of observing which teacher I have chosen must precede my decision to choose again. As The "Dynamics" of the Ego section in *A Course in Miracles* Chapter 11 reminds us:

> No one can escape from illusions unless he looks at them, for not looking is the way they are protected. There is no need to shrink from illusions, for they cannot be dangerous.

I believe this more and more as I remember to look.

> What is healing but the removal of all that stands in the way of knowledge? And how else can one dispel illusions except by looking at them directly, without protecting them?

On the floor by the door, Kayleigh woofs at an invisible enemy. I lift her to my face, eye-to-eye, hoping to reassure her. But somewhere in her DNA a wolf still reigns. She refuses to make eye contact with me, the dominant one in this position. I return her to her sentry post on the rug inside our garden door. She studies the glass, now and then barking at the many menacing forms her own shadow loves to take.

BOOKS

O is a symbol of the world, of oneness and unity. In different cultures it also means the "eye," symbolizing knowledge and insight. We aim to publish books that are accessible, constructive and that challenge accepted opinion, both that of academia and the "moral majority."

Our books are available in all good English language bookstores worldwide. If you don't see the book on the shelves ask the bookstore to order it for you, quoting the ISBN number and title. Alternatively you can order online (all major online retail sites carry our titles) or contact the distributor in the relevant country, listed on the copyright page.

See our website **www.o-books.net** for a full list of over 500 titles, growing by 100 a year.

And tune in to myspiritradio.com for our book review radio show, hosted by June-Elleni Laine, where you can listen to the authors discussing their books.

mySpiritRadio